When the Saints
Go Marching Out!

When the Saints
Go Marching Out!

Mobilizing the Church for Mission

ART BEALS

Geneva Press
Louisville, Kentucky

Scripture quotations from the New Revised Standard Version of the Bible are copyright © 1989 by the Division of Christian Education of the National Council of the Churches of Christ in the U.S.A. and are used by permission.

Scripture quotations marked NIV are from *The Holy Bible, New International Version.* Copyright © 1973, 1978, 1984 International Bible Society. Used by permission of Zondervan Bible Publishers.

Book design by Sharon Adams
Cover design by designpointinc.com

First edition

Published by Geneva Press
Louisville, Kentucky

This book is printed on acid-free paper that meets the American National Standards Institute Z39.48 standard. ♾

PRINTED IN THE UNITED STATES OF AMERICA

01 02 03 04 05 06 07 08 09 10 — 10 9 8 7 6 5 4 3 2 1

Library of Congress Cataloging-in-Publication Data is on file at the Library of Congress, Washington, D.C.

ISBN 0-664-50166-4

*To Sonia, my wife and life-partner, lover and best friend:
your loyalty and support have made these incredible
years of ministry fruitful, fulfilling, and fun!*

Contents

Foreword

by Bruce Larson

*I*n the middle of my ten-year term as senior pastor of University Presbyterian Church in Seattle, Art Beals joined our staff as pastor of urban and global missions. What an incredible resource he turned out to be. His energy is boundless, his worldwide contacts invaluable, his commitment to missions on every part of the globe unsurpassed, and his love for Jesus contagious.

By the time I left that post, over 10 percent of our three thousand members were engaged each year in long- or short-term missions. We learned that mission not only blesses those who are ministered to, but also blesses those who go to carry out Jesus' commission to "go into all the world and preach the gospel." I have personally seen hundreds of lives changed as lay people took that commission seriously and set out, on however short-term a basis, to be missionaries.

I am sure this brilliant book will challenge other churches to see every member as a potential missionary. It is a prophetic book about the church of tomorrow—which is here today in bits and pieces. Many churches have several pieces of this puzzle, but no one sees more of the complete picture than Art Beals, a missionary for Jesus to the world.

The church of tomorrow *is* here today and it is a church whose primary focus is mission and whose primary missionaries are lay men and women. Is it possible that we have come full circle to the New Testament church? This book holds forth that thrilling possibility.

Foreword

by Earl Palmer

*A*rt Beals is a Christian with God's love for the world on his heart and in his mind. He is a cross-cultural strategist who believes so strongly that the gospel of Jesus Christ is relevant and good that he has given his life to finding the people just over every fence so that they can discover for themselves God's grace. If you can find a barrier, Art Beals will find a door and a strategy for unlocking it. As a pastor, he has encouraged and trained ordinary Christians to enter into the cross-cultural world nearby and far away with equal urgency.

He is my friend, my teacher, and for ten years my colleague here at University Presbyterian Church in Seattle. During that partnership I watched a stream of Christian lay people young and old as they were prepared and deployed in practical ministries where they could make a concrete difference in the lives of people and for Jesus Christ's kingly reign.

His strategy as I see it is the model-of-hope strategy of the New Testament church lived forward into our contemporary world.

I urged Art Beals to write this book about saints who march out, and now at last here it is. Beware if you read this book, because this pastor has a way of getting under your skin and inside of your dreams!

Introduction

Dear Jane,

. . . And so, I am writing you this letter to end our engagement. Only recently have I fully understood your call to missionary service. When I asked you to marry me I was not aware of this very special commitment; maybe you were still unclear in your calling. And in no way do I want to discourage you or wish to stand in your way. I am equally certain that God has called me to prepare for the pastoral ministry here in the United States. I know that neither of us wishes to hinder in any way the other's commitment to fulfilling God's call. Jane, I have absolutely no plans to become a foreign missionary. . . . I must follow what I discern to be God's call for my life. For this reason and this reason alone I feel it best to end our relationship.

More than forty-eight years have passed since I wrote that letter. After our relationship ended, I completed my theological training, was ordained to the gospel ministry, married a wonderful woman who shared my vision for pastoral service, and became a pastor of a small but growing congregation in Washington State. However, six years later, several events prompted me to rethink my commitment to

American pastoral ministry. Thus began an incredible journey of more than forty-three years of missionary service and leadership (and sacrifice and support from Sonia, my home-loving wife). This service has taken me from Afghanistan to Zaire, sharing good news in more than a hundred countries. Each new mission experience has shaped my personal and family life and has added to my mission understanding.

God has a wonderful sense of humor! Jane began working for a publisher and eventually became a top corporate executive. She remained in the United States, and she never spent a single day in vocational missionary service! We were both so sincere in our understanding of God's call and our commitment to obey it. But neither of us really understood where that call and commitment might lead. I now understand that God's call primarily is to discipleship and obedience. This understanding opens a whole new universe of service and witness. God's call has very little to do with geography. It has to do with faith, with willingness to risk, with readiness to respond obediently to those challenges he places before us.

This book attempts to share what God is still teaching me about his call upon our lives and for his world. But first, I will retrace some of my own steps along the way.

One Defining Moment

I began the day by remaining at home longer than usual. The children were still sleeping and I lingered over a cup of coffee with my wife before heading off to the church office. On the radio, the Biola Hour aired in the background. Suddenly the announcer caught our attention with an urgent news bulletin: Five young missionary men were missing in Ecuador! He reported that they had been attempting a jungle meeting with unreached Indians, the

Aucas. I heard the name Jim Elliot, a high school class-mate of my brother in Portland, Oregon. I listened in stunned silence and thought of the wives and small children of these men. Sonia and I prayed for the men's safety and for God's comfort for their families. The story did not end as we had prayed and wished. In a very short time we learned that these five brave men had been murdered by the peo-ple they had worked diligently to befriend. Deep sorrow gripped our hearts. Five young men and their families had paid the ultimate price in order to share good news about a gift without price. Little did I know that their story would dramatically change my sense of calling and the life of my entire family.

The following weeks were filled with prayer, tears, and personal struggle. I tried to understand why their experi-ence was affecting me so deeply. Restless, I was losing some of my confidence in what I had believed was a life-long call to American pastoral ministry. I suspected that God was encouraging Sonia and me to take a fresh look at our lives, even though it didn't seem to make sense to change direction in my pastoral career. After all, I was far too encumbered with personal and ministry responsibili-ties to consider any changes. We had two children with a third one on the way. Besides, I had already settled that issue of missionary service through a broken engagement. Gently God began to give Sonia and me new understand-ing and fresh insights about our lives' direction. We shared a growing conviction about proclaiming the good news of Jesus Christ to those who had not yet heard.

More than a year later, God's call to missionary serv-ice became clear. After weeks of struggle, we filed appli-cations with three different mission agencies, not really expecting a response. No credible mission society would be interested in us; we were too old. (At age twenty-seven, I was facing my first midlife crisis!) Much to our surprise, all three mission agencies responded with interest. One proposed Indonesia as a field of service, another Japan, and the third suggested the Philippines. Following weeks of thoughtful prayer and guidance from those we knew to be wiser than ourselves, we committed to the agency with interest in the Philippines. Soon after, we were appointed to a ministry of evangelism and new church development. And on a very cold January morning in 1960, Sonia and I, with our three children, ages five, three, and one, sailed aboard a World War II freighter for what would become a lifelong career in mission service and leadership.

Evangelism and New Church Development

Our first ten years of missionary service were spent in evangelism and new church development in the Philippines with a mission agency primarily focused on rural and jungle ministries. While there, I became fascinated with a new challenge—the asphalt jungles of burgeoning urban populations in many African, Latin American, and Asian countries. With Western industrialization spreading ever more rapidly in these emerging countries, drastic population shifts followed the new industrial development of heretofore rural societies. Huge numbers of rural peasants were moving to the cities, lured by hopes of steady employment and expanded economic opportunity. Large slums arose across the landscape, changing these new urban centers forever. These migrant populations presented a remarkable new challenge for Christian ministry. Families were uprooted. Wives and children were often left behind in the villages while the men sought work. Village traditions and belief systems didn't seem to fit in with their new urban homes.

Here was a ministry challenge that stirred my pastor's heart! Practicing some of my pastoral skills and employing the new missiological insights of leaders such as

Eugene Nida, Donald McGavran, and Ralph Winter, I moved excitedly into a new style of urban mission and church development. Starting with a small group of Filipino professionals in a newly built suburb, we began to grow a church. Our first meeting place was a bakery, then we expanded to the beauty parlor next door. Using small-group principles and training new Filipino Christians in evangelistic home Bible study methods, the congregation grew rapidly. In a few years the congregation was empowered to build its own sanctuary and Christian education unit. A gifted Filipino electrical engineer became my ministry assistant. I promised to teach Fred Magbanua everything I knew about ministry if he would teach me everything I needed to know about the Philippines. In just five years I was able to step out of leadership and become Fred's assistant. He continued as pastor of this growing congregation for many years and went on to become a renowned world evangelical leader.

Decades later the congregation continues as a strong evangelical witness. Scores of new churches have developed under its tutelage and many of its most dedicated youth have served in cross-cultural ministries around the world. It was here that I developed my commitment to the local congregation and its essential role in cross-cultural ministry.

Discovering the Whole Gospel

I enjoy telling people about my church background. I was baptized at six weeks in my grandparents' Methodist church, my parents were converted soon afterward in an Aimee Semple McPherson revival meeting, and they reared me in the Foursquare Gospel Church. I grew up a pretty good kid, and never really rebelled during my teen years. Away from home while studying in a major Christian university, I finally rebelled by becoming a Baptist!

When people ask me why I then became a Presbyterian, I tell them that my income increased! All joking aside, each of these transitions was important in the professional and spiritual formation of my later years of ministry.

Growing up in a fundamentalist religious environment, I had a very strong commitment to evangelism but little understanding and much greater resistance to social ministries. Like many conservative Christians of my generation, I saw a great gulf between evangelism and social action. My ten years of Philippine ministry did little to change these viewpoints. However, upon returning to the United States and serving as pastor of a large downtown church in Portland, Oregon, I quickly discovered that I had not left the urban poor behind in Manila's slums. They were at the doorstep of my respectable middle-class downtown church. Learning how to serve them started a change in my life and my understanding of the gospel.

I remember preaching my first sermon that integrated the themes of evangelism and social concern: "God and Groceries!" During a home visit one week I discovered an elderly woman living in horrible circumstances. I was shocked to discover her eating from a can of dog food. It was the only meat she could afford. My fundamentalist background and my middle-class existence had not prepared me adequately for these new ministry challenges. I searched the scriptures for a fresh understanding. My desire to preach good news and to become good news grew in intensity daily. Once again I found myself rethinking my call.

I began to consider how I might be more actively involved in not just preaching the love of Christ, but finding new ways to demonstrate it. My ministry friends now included a group of evangelicals who were deeply concerned with helping the church recover its social conscience. We were concerned that the split between evangelism and social concern resulting from the modernist/fundamentalist controversies earlier in the century had influenced evangelical theology for too long. In time I resigned my pastorate and joined CRISTA Ministries in Seattle to develop one of its small ministries, Medicine for Missions, into a full-service evangelical relief and development organization. During the next ten years, Medicine for Missions was transformed into World Concern, a major Christian organization with a staff of more than three hundred professionals serving as Christ's witnesses among the poorest of the poor in scores of countries. My understanding and commitment to holistic ministry grew rapidly—the whole gospel to the whole world to help people become whole in Christ!

I was asked to cochair the Evangelism and Social Concern track at both Wheaton '83 and Lausanne II in Manila. These experiences further enlarged my understanding of the whole gospel and my network of international Christian friends and cherished ministry partners. This new decade of cross-cultural mission and service differed significantly from those spent in evangelism and new church development, yet it only strengthened my commitment to mobilizing gifted lay people for ministries of witness and service.

Back to the Local Congregation

I became physically exhausted by constant international travel demands. I was spending much of my life far from home and family, visiting personnel and projects and forming new ministry partnerships. But the professional restlessness that I was feeling was rooted in more than the accumulated fatigue of jet lag and mounting administrative frustrations. With my growing commitment to mobilizing lay people, I was eager to return to local congregation-centered ministry, where I could live out my passions and explore these strong convictions. At the time, Sonia and I were attending Seattle's University Presbyterian Church. Its senior pastor, Bruce Larson, had become a close personal friend. He served on my board of directors at World Concern International and we also shared in a weekly small group of seven men—known affectionately as The Seven Dwarfs! One day Bruce asked, "Art, what do you think it would look like if one congregation became fully mobilized for mission?" His question quickened my spirit and excited my imagination! Bruce's ministry was distinguished by his effectiveness in calling forth lay men and women to risk and follow their dreams, to discover their unique ministry gifts. Bruce's challenge merged with my desire for congregation-based ministry. Here was a healthy congregation fully committed to both mission and to lay ministry. No way could I resist the new challenge!

In the subsequent fifteen years, I have served this amazing congregation as pastor of urban and global mission. These years have been the most exciting, challenging, and rewarding years of my ministry to date. This congregation's experience in mission is the raw material for this book. From this ministry arose the privilege of helping the Presbyterian Church (U.S.A.)'s Division of Worldwide Ministries explore innovative approaches to cross-cultural ministry outreach. It is my fervent prayer that this book will help local congregations, both small and large, more effectively mobilize all of their lay people in effective cross-cultural ministry, first in their own geographical location, and then to the ends of the earth. With all my heart I believe that this mobilization in congregation-based mission provides the most effective option to fulfill Christ's words: "And this gospel of the kingdom will be preached in the whole world as a testimony to all nations" (Matthew 24:14).

1

Discovering a Place to Begin

*E*very new passion and conviction, every new idea, has to begin somewhere. For me it began with the martyrdom of the five young men in Ecuador, then was shaped by ten years of learning and doing mission in the Philippines. Ten more years of providing leadership for an international evangelical relief and development organization broadened my understanding of God's good news. These ministry experiences gave me valuable hands-on experience in vision setting and organizational development. Later, guiding a large urban congregation in local and global mission outreach greatly enhanced my understanding of many important missiological issues. None of these lessons were easy or without mistakes and disappointments. I discovered the need for one to develop the right starting place for the journey if one expects to arrive at the desired goal. My ministry goal was to enable a congregation to become fully mobilized for mission outreach and to create a model that would enable every congregation to discover its own effective cross-cultural ministry. Our biblical imperative is to make Christ fully known within every cultural setting, to make him known in a way that is both understandable and culturally responsible and relevant.

My starting place is the Word of God, and my understanding of it is informed and shaped by my own mission experiences and those of others. The biblical mandate is to "Go and make disciples of all nations."

The Father Initiated It

God's call to Abraham and to the holy nation Israel was actually a call to cross-cultural ministry. Through the consistent and faithful witness of the Hebrew nation, the entire world was to learn of the one true and living God. They were to be God's object lesson for the world. But the Hebrew people failed to claim their God-given purpose. Narrowly nationalistic and self-centered, they became content to quarrel over the finer points of religious doctrine and worship practices. In understanding their failure to proclaim and model the message of God's redemptive love and grace, one can more clearly understand the significance of the promise, "in the fullness of time God sent forth his only begotten Son." The Lord Jesus Christ came as God's very personal cross-cultural witness to a world possessing little or no understanding of God's redemptive ministry for his creation.

The Son Modeled It

Matthew's Gospel records one of the most remarkable histories of Jesus' mission to earth:

> Jesus went through all the towns and villages, teaching in their synagogues, preaching the good news of the kingdom and healing every disease and sickness. When he saw the crowds, he had compassion on them, because they were harassed and helpless, like sheep without a shepherd. Then he said to his disciples, "The harvest is plentiful but the workers are few. Ask the

Lord of the harvest, therefore, to send out workers into his harvest field." (Matthew 9:35–38)

Jesus proclaimed a simple yet profound missionary message of forgiveness, redemption, and cleansing. God came in Jesus Christ in order to reconcile a world bound by sin and desperately in need of restoration to him. The good news is that God's grace is greater than all of our sin. This message becomes central to all missionary activity. Jesus ministered to the total needs of the individual. His healing ministry always accompanied and often preceded his saving ministry. When he saw the people, harassed and helpless, scattered as sheep without a guiding shepherd, he was moved with compassion. He always responds to human need with divine compassion. His was no mere emotional response. His was an action response!

> Pity weeps and walks away;
> Compassion comes to help and stay.

Jesus, our cross-cultural missionary model, teaches us how to *live* in mission. He moves comfortably across cultural barriers when ministering to a Samaritan woman and a Roman centurion. He cleanses both lepers and harlots. He brings a message of hope for eternal life to both Nicodemus the religious zealot and to the dying thief on the cross. He brings light to the spiritually darkened and opens the eyes of the man born blind.

Jesus stops at the well at noonday and engages a Samaritan woman cross-culturally. He meets her on her home turf. He relates to her unique and very personal needs. He responds to her culture-bound questions. She seeks water. He offers living water. She yearns for deliverance from the guilt and accusations that are the natural outcome of a sinful lifestyle. He offers forgiveness. She feels deeply her own sense of condemnation. He offers grace. This grace changes her life forever! This would never have happened had Jesus been unwilling to cross the boundaries of culture that separated them.

Jesus' very brief public ministry demonstrates that we must be ready to risk. We must be ready to step outside our own particular personal comfort zones. We must believe that Jesus' redemptive ministry is a cross-cultural message to be shared with all.

The Holy Spirit Enables It

Following his resurrection and before he returns to the Heavenly Father, Jesus gives the disciples final instructions to remain in Jerusalem so that they might be prepared for a very special responsibility. He then promises them power that will make their cross-cultural witness effective. The book of Acts records this promise in action. The Holy Spirit was outpoured on the day of Pentecost in Jerusalem—a Jewish city where there were visitors from "every nation under heaven. . . . Parthians, Medes and Elamites; residents of Mesopotamia, Judea and Cappadocia, Pontus and Asia, Phrygia and Pamphylia, Egypt and the parts of Libya near Cyrene; visitors from Rome (both Jews and converts to Judaism); Cretans and Arabs" (Acts 2:5–11). On that first day of Pentecost, the Spirit's first work was to empower and enable those early disciples to communicate the good news of the risen Lord across all racial, ethnic, social, and religious boundaries.

To explain the Spirit's working, I turn back to a series of lectures I delivered some years ago at the Oxford Centre for Mission Studies. Developed from three different chapters of the book of Acts, these still express best both my missiological beliefs and ministry practices. I call these the three-legged stool forming my missiological understanding.

Act 1:
Not What We Really Planned For

In Acts 1, Jesus instructs his disciples, "Do not leave Jerusalem, but wait for the gift my Father promised. . . . For John baptized with water, but in a few days you will be baptized with the Holy Spirit" (Acts 1:4–5). In today's language, I believe Jesus is saying, "Don't *do* anything until you *become* something! Stay right where you are! You're not ready yet for the cross-cultural challenge! Don't run off half-cocked, but become adequately prepared for the ministry challenges you will face." This is excellent advice for those of us who are tempted to operate within our own power and limited resources. To wait for empowerment is especially important advice for those, who in their missiological zeal and activism, feel that they must hurry and complete the task now.

Not overly impressed with his advice, the disciples attempt to engage Jesus in a discussion concerning the end times: "Lord, are you at this time going to restore the kingdom to Israel?" (v. 6). People of vastly different cultures share an interest, even a fascination, with the idea that there must be a terminal point in history. The shelves of Christian bookstores are filled with attempts at correlating current history with the particular author's own prophetic speculations. By not answering directly, Jesus seems to imply that they are asking the wrong question: "It is not for you to know the times or dates the Father has set by his own authority" (v. 7). There is an important missiological lesson here. The burning issue in mission is not to finish the job, but to remain faithful to the task. Our propensity toward grandiosity in our carefully planned mission outreach strategies must be tempered by this truth. Our commitment to strategic planning takes on a whole new and richer context when we understand this basic ministry principle.

Then follows a mission text, which is the theme for many mission conferences: "But you will receive power when the Holy Spirit comes on you; and you will be my witnesses in Jerusalem, and in all Judea and Samaria, and to the ends of the earth" (v. 8). Rightly understood, this is not merely a statement of Jesus' command or commission to the church. Rather, it is more a statement of *cause* and *effect*. The cause is the empowerment of the Holy Spirit in our lives. The effect is that this Spirit-empowerment equips and frees the church for cross-cultural ministry. All Christians are called to cross-cultural ministry. The most profound cross-cultural call we can possibly receive is to follow Jesus and become part of the kingdom of God. His kingdom presents a whole new culture of ideas, values, behaviors, and priorities. These are often diametrically opposite to the prevailing values of our own culture. Only as we are filled with God's Holy Spirit do we develop the capacity to exchange our false cultural values for the values of the kingdom of God. This is the enabling power of the Holy Spirit, which must be experienced if we are to be effective in cross-cultural mission service.

Act 2:
Not What We Really Expected

Later chapters in the book of Acts record the history of this emerging and growing church. Since its rather dramatic beginnings on the day of Pentecost, the Jerusalem church has now become well established and severely persecuted: "A great persecution broke out against the church at Jerusalem, and all except the apostles were scattered throughout Judea and Samaria" (8:1). As a direct result of this scattering, the Jerusalem church now multiplies in other cities and districts of the area. The church in Antioch was established at this time. However, not until a second wave of persecution grips the church do we see it move out in mission. "Now those who had been scattered by the persecution in connection with Stephen traveled as far as Phoenicia, Cyprus and Antioch, telling the message only to Jews" (11:19). This is just as Jesus had promised his first disciples. They did not know then what instrument the Sovereign God would employ to spread the gospel, only that when they were empowered for ministry they would be released to go. The Holy Spirit's role in mission outreach now becomes more understandable. Mission requires the ability to survive while going. The empowerment of the Spirit is essential.

The church's empowerment by the Spirit brings fresh insights into important principles of healthy missiology.

1. The church must become cross-cultural in its makeup before it successfully becomes cross-cultural in its outreach. Scripture powerfully witnesses to this truth: "Men from Cyprus and Cyrene went to Antioch and began to speak to Greeks also" (Acts 11:20). This event had been foretold to Peter in the vision he received in the house of Cornelius. But it took believers open to the Spirit's leading to translate this vision into an action plan. People of one culture travel to another culture to discover a people of a third culture needing to hear the message of salvation!

2. Before proclaiming God's good news in a new location, always stop long enough to observe what God has been doing before the missionary arrives! "Some of them . . . began to speak to Greeks also, telling them the good news about the Lord Jesus. The Lord's hand was with them, and a great number of people believed and turned to the Lord" (Acts 11:20–21). These Greek citizens of Antioch were ready and ripe to receive the gospel, and the newly arrived "men from Cyprus and Cyrene" saw what God had been preparing before they arrived. Here were

Greek citizens yearning to receive good news heretofore proclaimed only to Jews! We need to discover how to fit into what God is already doing or preparing.

3. It is significant to note that "the disciples were called Christians first at Antioch." The presence and the empowerment of the Holy Spirit at Antioch enabled the church to break out of its monocultural existence. Never again would the true religion of Abraham, Isaac, and Moses be merely a nationalistic religion concerned with its own deity. Christianity has become a universal faith! And, at the dawn of the third millennium, its followers are now gathered from every race, language, and nation.

Act 3:
Not Necessarily What We Were Prepared to Do

Observe one more step in the formation of the early Christian church. God begins to form his new missionary force, starting with two unlikely candidates—a newly converted Jew and a foreign Gentile from Cyprus! Saul, soon to be renamed Paul, and Barnabas are now appointed and commissioned by this church in Antioch to leave the geographical and cultural limits of Judea and Samaria and spread the good news (Acts 13:1–3). They travel first to the island nation of Cyprus, then to the Roman province of Asia. Later Paul and others would take the gospel to Europe—the early beginnings of transmitting the Christian message to the ends of the earth.

Observe two very important missiological insights. First, the Holy Spirit empowers every church to spread the message of Christ's saving and transforming power to the ends of the earth. "The church exists for mission as fire exists by burning!" Act 3 becomes the fulfillment of Jesus' promise in act 1.

Second, the biblical model for mission has its basis in

the congregation—not a mission agency, not a parachurch ministry, and not a denominational bureaucracy. Mission structures can help congregations develop mission vision and implement mission strategies, but the local congregation is God's starting point. Any congregation that neglects this task is being less than what God has called it to be. Any organization that misunderstands the local congregation, marginalizes its importance, or bypasses its spiritual authority ceases to be faithful to the missionary task entrusted first to the local church. At Antioch, the congregation became the first mission society. Local congregational leaders identified and then commissioned their own volunteers for mission outreach. They provided resources for these mission volunteers. They supported them with their prayers and encouragement. The church at Philippi sent Epaphroditus as a short-term missioner to provide special assistance to Paul, the missionary already serving in the field. And the sending church required accountability from the missionary upon return from field service.

The local church as mission agency is an idea that is two thousand years old. Yet a cursory study of mission history demonstrates that for centuries those most committed to world mission often ignored the local congregation, and, tragically, many local congregations were not at all prepared to accept their own responsibility in mission outreach. Therefore, it should not be surprising that in Protestant mission history, mission boards, agencies, and societies became the center for both the planning and implementation of missionary activity. Until recently, the local church provided an ever diminishing or nonexistent role in guiding cross-cultural mission outreach. Local churches were appreciated for being the source for recruiting missionaries, and they were relied upon to provide financial resources. Seldom, however, were they included in planning and developing mission strategies. Now with the advent of modern communication and transportation, local congregations are no longer satisfied to remain at the periphery of mission planning and implementation. With the phenomenal growth of larger congregations, this tendency to marginalize local church mission involvement has diminished. Increasingly, the local congregation is valued as a full partner with mission agencies and societies in implementing shared mission visions and strategies.

The local congregation should be recognized as the center for mission planning, mobilization, and outreach. Then various noncongregational mission structures can ably assist the church in implementing its mission mandate. No local body of believers has all the historical perspective, the support, and experience necessary to faithfully implement God's missionary call. In no way does this principle marginalize valid mission structures. Rather, it authenticates their reason for existence. True partnerships involve local congregations with other mission structures and denominational organizations along with mission partners formed in the field of ministry. These partnerships will assist each partner in implementing Christ's missionary mandate and make the ministry outcomes more effective and long lasting.

What works for the large congregation is just as relevant for small churches. A small church has even fewer resources to implement mission than its large counterparts. However, within its people it has the same potential for mission planning, mobilization, and outreach. Through developing active partnerships with other local congregations, small and large, or with local presbyteries or other such groups, the small church has both the responsibility and the opportunity to implement its congregation-based outreach ministries.

At University Presbyterian Church, as our mission program has grown, rather than becoming more independent in our mission activities, we have become more interdependent with outside mission structures and organizations. In India, our partnership with the Divya Shanti organization helped us develop some of our local mission leaders while helping our Indian partners develop further some of their ministry resources. We have sent our interns to their programs in Bangalore, and have received their interns in Seattle to learn the many aspects of ministry in a local congregation. In Russia we have successfully worked with Russian Orthodox congregations, with the Orthodox Seminary in Saint Petersburg, and with Orthodox Church leaders to strengthen their local ministries of evangelism, education, and social concern. In Albania, a ministry partnership with InterVarsity and the International Fellowship of Evangelical Students gives leadership in developing a national student ministry. We have served in partnership with the United Bible Society to facilitate interconfessional cooperation in supplying and distributing scriptures. We have partnered with the Orthodox Church of Albania, providing assistance in English language training and in various diaconal ministries.

In each of these examples, our congregation has provided qualified personnel to help develop these ministries. We have demonstrated that we can accomplish together what we could never accomplish alone. The task of world evangelization in a cross-cultural context is a tough assignment. It cannot be done apart from the call, the blessing, and the empowerment of Almighty God. And it cannot be effectively accomplished without the deliberate and intentional cooperation between local congregations and larger mission organizations and structures. Whatever form these partnerships may take, the combined vision, energy, and resources of these partnerships will propel the task of world evangelization forward.

2

Converting Your Mission Statement into an Action Plan

*A*rt and Eloise registered for our church's adult education series, "Becoming a World Christian," an eight-week course designed to deepen members' understanding of God's missionary purposes and stimulate interest in mission service. In class each week I sensed their growing spirit of adventure and excitement. I eagerly awaited their request for an appointment with me that they might share their excitement and ministry dreams.

That day soon came. They told me their professional backgrounds and provided pertinent information regarding their personal spiritual journeys, their current life situation, and their interest in exploring a future mission assignment where their interests and professional skills and experiences could be useful. Art was in his early fifties and had spent a very active and successful career as a public school teacher, athletic coach, and school administrator. He also had served on several government-sponsored educational commissions. In addition, he was a very informed theologian. Complementing his undergraduate work at Whitworth College and a doctorate in educational administration at Columbia University, he also held a master of divinity degree from Princeton University. Art was restless in both his personal and professional life. Eloise was currently teaching English as a second language (ESL) in the public school system. The previous summer Eloise had linked up with one of our short-term mission teams and had taught ESL to public school teachers in Kyrgyzstan. She received a great deal of pleasure and developed a high level of mission awareness and potential career interest from her summer's ministry.

At this time I had two very urgent service opportunities for our work in Albania, opportunities that needed their types of skills. Several years earlier, in partnership with other Albania mission groups, we founded an urgently needed missionary school. The school's headmaster had recently resigned and an experienced educator and administrator was desperately needed. Art perfectly fit the bill. Our ministry partners in Albania's Orthodox Church had asked us to find a mission volunteer to assist with their English language training program for Orthodox seminarians and lay members. This need was a great match for Eloise's skills. The couple resigned from their public school posts and were on their way to new careers that combined their mission interests and professional experience.

Mission Must Be Informed by Purpose

After Art and Eloise started serving in their new challenging ministries in Albania, I reflected on the steps that had led them from enrollment in an adult education class to engaging in a fulfilling new career. Without the church's mission commitment and leadership, they would probably still be serving with professional excellence in their school district while feeling spiritually unfulfilled. It took years of our church's investment to make a mission assignment like this possible. Why did our congregation invest so fully in building a mission strategy and developing the resources to implement it? How had we learned to help members dream great ministry dreams, to risk much to serve the kingdom of God? I reached up and took from the shelf a copy of the *Mission Handbook* of University Presbyterian Church (UPC). The answer was on the first page of this two-hundred-page mission leadership manual in our Statement of Purpose:

The Department of Urban and Global Mission's purpose is to plan and supervise the development and deployment of human, financial and partnership resources for cross-cultural ministry opportunities locally, nationally and globally. It fulfills this purpose by performing the following functions:

1. Lead the congregation in developing a strategic focus for the congregation's involvement in urban and global evangelization and discipleship training.

2. Educate the congregation regarding all aspects of a scriptural understanding of cross-cultural mission outreach.

3. Provide mission information, education and motivation to the congregation in order to stimulate full and increased support for all facets of UPC's cross-cultural mission outreach ministries.

4. Provide cross-cultural mission counsel and support to all UPC departments in order to assist them in implementing their mission outreach objectives.

5. Provide career counseling to UPC members, enabling them to discover short-term, career and post-retirement mission service opportunities.

6. Develop spiritual and material resources for the support of UPC-sponsored local, national and global mission personnel, national scholars and workers, and mission projects.

7. Provide cross-cultural orientation and training opportunities in order to equip UPC members for mission outreach service.

8. Provide counsel and pastoral support to all

UPC-sponsored mission personnel serving in field assignments.

9. Develop local, national and global networks for the purpose of mission partnership formation.

10. Develop creative opportunities for urban mission involvement through the development and maintenance of approved UPC-supported residential communities.

11. Provide mission counsel and support to individual churches, denominational and selected mission parachurch organizations when consistent with UPC's program objectives.

There it was! We were seeing our mission plan implemented! The investment of the time, talents, and resources of many of our church members caused our mission strategy to become a reality in the lives of this couple and in the lives of our Albanian friends. That is not to say that our plan is perfect or that we carry it out with anything resembling perfection. But it holds out our ideals and provides a framework for helping present and future missioners find God's plan for sharing their lives cross-culturally. Then when field conditions change, as they did for Art and Eloise and as they do for most of us, there is support for the mission worker's effort to hear God's call above the chaos.

Permeating Plans
with Philosophy and Purpose

How does such a plan come about? I remember hearing a young boy's comment after he had run terrified into his waiting mother's arms, fleeing the threatening snarls and barks of a vicious dog: "I was so scared, Mama, that I ran all directions at once!" Sometimes I get the feeling that church programs reflect this same action plan in trying to meet very difficult challenges. There is so much that needs to be done, so many choices in how and where to do it. We just don't know where to begin! But we all begin somewhere. Working together to first develop a congregation's statement of purpose is a great place to begin. Purpose needs to precede planning. Prudent reflection on our shared values, beliefs, and priorities will inform our actions. Challenging all of our stated and unstated assumptions will help more clearly develop a clear philosophy for congregational mission involvement. Your church's mission plan should not mirror UPC's or anyone else's, no matter how theoretically appealing. God has given your church its own firsthand learning experiences.

With that in mind, I offer some scripturally sound guidelines developed by Dr. Timothy Dearborn, my predecessor here at UPC and a leading thinker in mission circles. In a paper entitled, "The Essential Elements of a Congregational-Based Cross-Cultural Ministry," he lists seven qualities that help define a successful congregation-based mission program. These distinguishing qualities are:

> Relational
> Reciprocal
> Intentional
> Kingdom-centered
> Comprehensive
> Supernatural
> Joyously costly

These elements regularly inform our congregation's mission purposes, its programs, and partnership relationships. Consider incorporating them into your own mission plan.

Relational. The kingdom of God is knit together by a vast web of relationships. The church is more than an institution or an organization filled with knowledge and activities. One of the mysteries of the church is that God is blending his people together, growing them into the people of God, the body of Christ. Jesus did not die to redeem programs but to redeem individuals. The church was not formed to create lone rangers but to create redemptive communities. If our ministries are to be effective, they must be relational. Effective personal relationships are essential. Building support groups for both lay volunteers and field workers provides that opportunity for relationship building. Creating lay task forces around a shared vision, ideas, and concerns binds interested participants together.

Our mission department has been transformed by eliminating traditional committees and replacing them with small communities—task forces—tightly organized around very specific interests and program goals. These task forces continue only as long as the relationships remain healthy and the ministry goals are kept fresh and challenging. When groups and task forces meet we encourage them to provide opportunities for both prayer and sharing. Each member is given an opportunity to share his or her own life story. *What was my life like as a child? How did Christ become real in my life? What special mission concern invites my attention? What personal or family concerns am I now experiencing that my small group or support team can help me with or pray for?* Sharing answers to questions like these builds that special sense of community and imparts deeper meaning to the task around which they are organized.

Reciprocal. We are called to be in mission with Christ's global church. Within these partnerships we experience reciprocity: We learn to become receivers as well as givers, learners as well as teachers, listeners as well as speakers. Effective mission service, whether short-term or career, succeeds best when these values permeate every relationship. We can give no greater gift to others than extending to them the opportunity of giving back to us. This has been a difficult lesson for me to learn. Sometimes my need to give is rooted in my need to prove my own self-worth. Because of my Protestant work ethic and my Depression-era mentality, I have expended much energy serving others but have often been insensitive to their desires to serve me. It has been easier to be generous with my possessions than to allow others to share with me. The key to understanding reciprocity in relationships is found in the words of our Savior: "Freely you have received, freely give."

Intentional. Our congregation has developed both a national and international reputation for its commitment to mission. The mailbox and the e-mail inbox are regularly filled with requests from missionary candidates soliciting help in developing their financial support base. Indigenous church leaders, national churches, and parachurch ministries supply us with fresh opportunities for financial participation in their projects. Sometimes these are full of interesting challenges and at other times they appear to present some enterprising person's latest fundraising idea! How do mission leaders make critical choices about which opportunities to support? After all, no one person or organization can do everything. But we can do something! Intentionality in decision making implies both vision and focus. A mission program must be infused with purpose, focus, and direction. Otherwise the congregation will be tempted to contribute something to every need that comes to its attention. We must possess an unshakable conviction for those tasks that God has called us to perform. Then we need to remain focused on those tasks.

Select a few strategic projects or begin by supporting one or two new missionaries or national workers chosen by lay workers who already contribute their own resources to these activities or individuals. Then enlarge your number of projects or supported individuals as more of the laity become involved in those programs they wish to support. The small church can be every bit as enterprising in its ministries and as strategic in its outreach as any large congregation.

Our congregation's focus was sharpened by the vision of one young man. Dave grew up with parents who were Presbyterian missionaries serving in Iran. They were killed in an automobile accident while on furlough in the Midwest. Thus ended Dave's Iranian experience but not his love for Muslims and his desire to share Christ's redeeming love with them. Several years ago Dave came to our monthly department meeting with a challenge for us to critically evaluate our current commitment to Muslim mission outreach. He was convinced that we were not adequately prioritizing or focusing our resources to meet the challenge of Islam, the religion followed by one of every five persons in the world. Passionately convinced that every Muslim brother and sister deserves to hear God's message of grace in a context that is respectful and culturally appropriate, Dave pointed out that Muslims were the most underevangelized "people group." Many mission organizations and evangelistic strategies are ill-equipped to respond to this challenge. We were a bit chagrined when he pointed out that in the previous five years less than one half of 1 percent of our missionary funds were specifically targeted for this urgent ministry need. We were not fully aware of this fact because we had never set any priorities for Muslim ministry. We listened carefully. Dave suggested that we form a task force composed of lay members who shared Dave's ministry concern. We would empower them to study the issue, prepare a report, and bring back specific recommendations.

When the task force submitted its report, it proposed increasing our funding for Muslim ministry from the current one half of 1 percent to 25 percent—and in just five years' time! The challenge made us feel like a person taking his automobile into the dealership for repair and then saying, "I need my car's motor overhauled but I can't turn the engine off!" Major adjustments would be necessary if we were to respond to this challenge. It is often easier to avoid new opportunities for intentional ministry by just doing what we have always done. It is painfully difficult to make significant program changes and to reprioritize funding. There is a great amount of loyalty and a high sense of ownership over each person's favorite mission project or missionary. In the process of change there is always something to give up in order to receive something in exchange that is new.

We listened and learned, talked and strategized. Our very best mission advocates made difficult changes in order to reach new strategic goals. A few found the changes so painful that they shifted their involvement to other areas of our church and even to other churches. Confident that God's direction for us had come through Dave's challenge, we made the changes—a few the first year, more in later years. Today we celebrate those changes. Financial resources available for mission outreach have increased at least fivefold. Ten years after Dave's initial challenge, nearly 68 percent of our million-dollar mission budget is invested in Muslim ministries!

Kingdom-Centered. "Jesus went everywhere preaching the good news of the kingdom of God." This kingdom message is concerned equally with regeneration of the human heart and uplifting of the circumstances surrounding each individual's human existence. To become committed to kingdom-centered mission will, by the very nature of our understanding, cause us to become more holistic in our ministry outreach. Our program values must respond to the full spectrum of human need: physical, socioeconomic, mental, and spiritual. Our ministry priorities need to be balanced between evangelism and social concern. Our missionary message will reflect both the love of God and the justice of God. Our witness will call both for personal repentance from sinfulness and corporate repentance from the collective evil in social and economic structures. Our missionary mandate is not so much a call to build the church—this is Christ's own responsibility—but to build his kingdom. This is what it means to be kingdom-centered. As we hurry to proclaim good news to a hurting world we must run on both legs of the gospel—evangelism and social concern. By running on both of these legs we learn to persevere. The effective congregation-based mission program extends both hands of the gospel to those it serves. And the gospel truly becomes good news!

For more than fifteen years Bruce has served the impoverished people of northeastern Haiti with a kingdom-centered ministry. This young missionary pioneer is equally prepared to lead a Bible study or to dig ditches and lay water pipe. Shortly after his arrival in Haiti, Bruce astutely observed the problem of thirst among the people he was committed to serve. Their thirst was spiritual, and they longed for that living water that only God can give. But he also saw their thirst for clean drinking water and for water to refresh their animals and irrigate their crops. Bruce's ministry was located in the most drought-prone area of Haiti. Most of the villages were without any convenient source of either living water or the liquid kind. Through innovative food-for-work projects he enlisted the enthusiastic participation of hundreds of villagers who agreed to dig ditches and lay pipe in exchange for food for their children. Child malnourishment was epidemic in this area.

Bruce's vision and commitment have summoned the talents and resources of scores of our laity who volunteer on short-term mission assignments to help him accomplish his ministry goals. Clean and cool drinking water flows today in those villages. Many children now avoid the water-borne diseases most destructive to their health. Parents are spared the sorrow of burying their own children. Churches have sprung up in the fertile soil of communities whose residents gladly received living water after Bruce saw their need for drinking water.

Comprehensive. We need to involve the entire congregation in mission outreach. Each Sunday I look out across the congregation and try to visualize individual interests and skills. These become the raw material for developing a mission strategy that can most effectively engage the resources of our congregation. By identifying these resources we can explore every possible partnership with churches and organizations that share our concerns for reaching our world with Christ's love. Our approach is comprehensive because we are committed to engage in mission at every appropriate level available to us: congregation, denomination, mission society, parachurch agency, national churches, and international mission structures. Mission is the task for all the people of God and it is far too important to trust to the hands of just a few mission specialists. Living in mission, our hearts beat with the heart of God!

Supernatural. It is not by the might of great mission organizations, nor by the power of our efforts no matter how talented we might be, but by the power of God's Spirit that we are equipped to engage in mission. Cross-cultural outreach is a difficult task, far too difficult to accomplish on our own. We soon discover that we labor not against flesh and blood but against principalities and powers—evil powers in high places—and we desperately need supernatural power. No matter how large our church or mission, no matter how plentiful its resources and opportunities for ministry, without the power of God at work in our lives, advantages will add up to very little. The Christian community's growth is not dependent upon our power to persuade or to plan. Quite the opposite: Our missionary efforts succeed most when clothed in humility and weakness. Our mission successes will be measured more by our faithfulness than by their fruitfulness. Full trust in and reliance upon the Supernatural One is an essential part of mission engagement.

Joyously costly. In my years of ministry and mission consulting, I have observed an abundance of joyless labor. Quarrels over the mission department's budget share replace the joy we can share from the abundance of skills and talents available within our congregations. Committees often exhaust themselves in staging mission conferences that too few attend. Because so many of our mission efforts are implemented far from home, often unnoticed and unappreciated, we feel unnecessary. Discouragement can overwhelm any of us when we lose our focus or fail to consider the cost of mission service. However, give me a group of lay people deeply committed and involved in fulfilling their dreams for mission service and I will show you an excited and joyous group of people! I don't suggest that everything is fun. None of us find pleasure in every difficult task, but much that is of lasting value in mission is joyously costly! While paying an enormous cost for his service, Paul presented joy-filled mission reports to those churches that sent him. Hear his witness to the church in Thessalonica concerning that costly element of ministry: "We were delighted to share with you not only the gospel of God but our lives as well" (1 Thessalonians 2:8). Don't be too quick to engage in mission service without first considering the price. Guide your volunteers and mission leaders to do the same. More than fads, feelings, and facts must permeate our mission planning.

Before moving outward, journey inward. Identify those values that are consistent with Christ's kingdom call. Permit those values to inform all decisions your congregation makes in implementing its mission outreach. Mission service can be costly, but under the Lordship of Jesus Christ it remains joyously costly. It demands our very best! It calls for sacrificial giving and sacrificial obedience. Sometimes, as in the case of those five young men in Ecuador, it may even demand our lives.

3

Developing a Theology of Vocation

*C*hristians in healthy, growing churches understand that God's kingdom ministry has been entrusted to the *laos*—the people of God: "But you are a chosen people, a royal priesthood, a holy nation, a people belonging to God, that you may declare the praises of him who called you out of darkness into his wonderful light" (1 Peter 2:9). There are now significant ways in which lay people are understood as full participants in ministry and leadership. It is lay men and women who are connected daily to the nonbeliever in their workplace or in the marketplace. These are the ones most fluent in the language of heart and mind. The laity are the most compelling evidence that good news works for average people!

"God Loves You . . . and Art Beals Has a Wonderful Plan for Your Life!"

Several years ago one of our associate pastors remarked in a sermon, "I don't know what happens in Art Beals's office. It's a big black hole! People go in there and they are never seen again!" The congregation laughed and people nodded to one another, recalling friends who had indeed disappeared, only to turn up later returning from a mission assignment.

Our congregation commissions for missionary service hundreds of individuals and many teams every year. These public commissionings are a priority in our worship services. The whole church family becomes the missioner's support team, providing friendship, prayers, and financial resources. There is a variety of mission assignments: Short-term mission Journey teams are sent out by our adult ministries department, and hundreds of youth and their adult sponsors participate in a house-building project in Mexico or summer missions to migrant farm workers near to home. Our university ministries department involves scores of students each summer in a World Deputation ministry. This fifty-year program has now fielded more than thirteen hundred students, an impressive number of these transitioning later into formal mission careers and many more assuming important lay leadership roles. Many more individuals expand our mission outreach by providing skilled and professional leadership where special jobs need just the right volunteer.

Another of our pastors observed, "I fully expect that some day when Art Beals is preaching, as we exit our sanctuary we will see a whole fleet of buses lined up outside the church's doors. They will be waiting to whisk off the whole congregation for some mission experience! And an added benefit in their going is that this will help solve our parking problem!" This may be an exaggeration but not an altogether untrue accusation. Our congregation experiences great delight in seeing friends discover their own unique place of service. One of our members coined a humorous saying that reflects rather honestly what people think—"God loves you. . . . and Art Beals has a wonderful plan for your life!"—as if I were some demigod or divine sergeant at arms grabbing unwilling people to travel to undesirable places, unprepared for ministry, in order to serve against their will!

Discerning the Call

My secretary once taught me a valuable lesson when she overheard me complaining about my carelessness in misplacing something. From her adjoining office she said, "Art, don't be so hard on yourself. There are only three in the Trinity and you're not one of them!" Her advice has helped me in ways she didn't plan. I am often tempted to be too hard on myself. However, her words also bear great wisdom when it comes to giving others vocational guidance. Making plans for another's life is risky business. If the plan succeeds, the source of the wisdom is forgotten. If the advice fails, the person never forgets the wisdom that led her astray! A Christian community provides people with a network of relationships that can assist them in discerning God's call. These friends will know our strengths and weaknesses. They can best validate our giftedness and guide us when we misjudge our own self-worth. In the end, I am not really interested in convincing anybody to do anything. I want to help people discover who they are, what their special gifts and skills might be, and then assist them in discerning God's special call for them. One of the most exciting parts of ministry is to assist others in processing the implications of God's call upon their lives, to help them broaden their horizons, increase vocational options, dream new possibilities—to open up new avenues of ministry to those processing God's call upon their life and service.

I find that an important part of my ministry is accomplished through counseling individuals about their vocational or ministry options. Some are experiencing a very important crossroad in life. This crossroad may involve a posteducation or a postretirement decision. They may be disinterested in their current vocation, or they may be earnestly seeking to find something vocationally that will fill them with a greater sense of purpose than they experience in their current career. Some are university students who are facing graduation but remain uncertain about a future career. They are not yet ready to settle down but are interested in giving one or two years to a specialized ministry. Their desire to serve in cross-cultural ministry has been limited by the pressures of their studies. Other counselees are either retired or considering an early retirement. They have no desire to become inactive nor do they need to earn more personal income. They are interested in investigating a vocational opportunity that is consistent with their vocational background but provides a ministry challenge that they have not been able to pursue before. Still others are young professionals burned out by all-consuming high-pressure careers. Many young professionals feel unfulfilled in careers that others would deem successful. Vocational restlessness can be an opportunity to ask some of the more important value-oriented questions that many miss the opportunity to ask when first entering a career.

Five Key Vocational Questions

I begin a typical vocational inquiry by first asking the individual to share with me his personal story: *Tell me a little about your childhood and family background. How did Christ become real in your life? What is of special importance in your life right now? How is God making himself real to you daily?* Most people relish telling stories of the people and events that were formative in their lives. After they have done so I have a sense of who they are and where their interest lies. When I am sure that they have come to either investigate or plan some new vocational options, I then ask five basic vocational questions:

1. What do you want to do?
2. Why do you want to do it?

3. Where do you want to do it?
4. How long do you want to do it?
5. What are the results you hope to achieve from this decision?

Although these are very simple, nondirective questions, they will help the inquirer focus her vocational thoughts, reveal her ministry aspirations, and thus inform her process of decision making. The sequence of the questions is intentional:

Question 1 is a nondirective question of *vocation.*
Question 2 explores the individual's *motivation.*
Question 3 helps the individual discover the possibilities of *location.*
Question 4 sets the time *limitation.*
Question 5 identifies and focuses the *expectation.*

Many of us bring a lot of negative baggage with us when we consider new directions for either vocation or volunteer service. Somehow we have grown up believing that following God's will is often very unpleasant or, at the least, unnatural. While maturing in Christ we often cling to very immature ideas about God's will, believing it to be unpleasant, inconvenient, or unrelated to who we are or what we desire to do. But when people thoughtfully answer these questions, the excitement is palpable.

Paul's words in Romans 12 are instructive in helping us to understand how to make wise vocational choices. Consider this challenge:

1. *Discover the new life.* In view of God's mercy, we offer our lives to him for service and witness. We find that special place, that new life, not by imitating or conforming to the world and

its values, but through transformation of our inner lives. Such transformation is focused on our minds; therefore, in order to discover God's will we first need to get our thinking straight! (Romans 12:1–2a)

2. *Discover God's will.* Transformed minds will help us test and confirm what is
   • *pleasant* (Now that's a switch! I thought the will of God was always unpleasant!)
   • *pleasing* (not to God, but to us! God is already pleased with us. He calls us his beloved and he wants his will to be pleasing to us.
   • *perfect* (God's will has integrity. It fits consistently with who we are [v. 2b].)

3. *Discover your true self.* It is always safe to look at ourselves when we search through the lens of God's grace. In making vocational decisions we need to be delivered from our grandiosity. Honest reflection and sober judgment will keep us humble. This judgment is made possible by the measure of faith God has given us (v. 3).

4. *Discover your community.* The church of Jesus Christ is God's gift, given so that no one will ever again have to operate independently. We will best discern our call when it is validated and affirmed by our special community (vv. 4–5).

5. *Discover your giftedness.* The New Testament provides us with a long list of spiritual gifts in Romans 12, 1 Corinthians 12, and Ephesians 4, which embrace the giftedness of us all.

Our negative religious experiences often interfere in our believing that God really has our best interests at heart. Yet God is the Lord of Creation; he knows how he has made us, how we best function, what turns us on. He blesses us with gifts and talents, and he rejoices when we develop these for the glory of God *and* for our own personal enjoyment. Our created uniqueness is enhanced by our vocational development. Our interests and desires merge together and assist us in discovering special mission service opportunities. Volunteer mission service, whether short-term or career, are not simply temporary career diversions. In them we explore new ministry opportunities that are personally fulfilling and that honor Christ. We do not have to trash who we are in order to become what God wishes us to be!

Moses clearly understood the implausibility of his preparedness to lead the people of God. But he is encouraged by the Lord's inquiry: "Moses, what is that in your hand?" Moses understood it merely as a rod to guide sheep, but God empowered him to use it to guide God's people through their wilderness experience. Wise vocational choices always build the future on what is in our hands today. Sensible vocational guidance helps us discern our calling and identify our strengths and gifts, which then can be effectively used in kingdom witness and service.

Scuba Diving for Christ

I am not often stumped by the modesty or unawareness of a vocational inquirer who feels she has nothing of vocational value on which to build a life for mission service. One such young woman came to me for vocational guidance one day. Jan's desire was to serve God cross-culturally but was certain that she had nothing to qualify her for this type of vocational call. There was a tug in her heart for overseas mission service, but she thought there was nothing in her educational or vocational experiences that could possibly qualify her for the desired ministry opportunity. She wanted to serve in a difficult place where the gospel had not yet penetrated. This desire caused her to consider ministry to Muslims, but her personal and vocational history gave her nothing to validate her desires. Jan was confused in feeling that God would give her desires so contrary to her gifts. After listening to her story and her vocational aspirations, I asked her the five basic questions. She attempted a response to each question, but her responses were hesitating and timid.

"I know I have a real heart for people of the Muslim faith," she asserted. "For some time I have believed that God was calling me to serve them. But I have absolutely nothing in my vocational background or my current career—no outstanding skills, no special training, nothing that would seem to be of any real value in preparing for service in a Muslim country. About all I have is my desire to go, to make friends, and then to quietly share my faith."

I was stumped. Nothing in Jan's answers summoned my slumbering creativity. She had an accurate understanding of her limited vocational experiences and professional skills that would suggest no easy course of action. Her chosen vocation and her current career path just did not provide what is usually needed for mission service. All that Jan had been doing vocationally was good, but nothing seemed to fit conveniently into where she wanted to go and what she wanted to do. In answering the location question, she had quickly identified Africa as her first choice of where to live and serve. Knowing no other questions and responding to a divine hunch, I asked her if she had any hobbies. With that question she really came alive!

"Oh yes. I love scuba diving. In fact I am a licensed scuba diving instructor!" She seemed a bit embarrassed by her quick response. It seemed impossibly separate from the rest of our discussion. She had made her appointment to share a deep concern for Muslims and for Africa, not to discuss hobbies! What possible relevance could scuba diving have to do with sharing God's love with others?

I promised Jan that I would think further about her situation. We set an appointment in another two weeks. When she was gone I reflected on our conversation, concluding that she probably was as ill-equipped in her training and vocational experience as she seemed to feel. But Jan did have a real heart for God! She demonstrated a consistent Christian witness, regularly sharing her faith with others. Jan had prepared herself as well as she could by attending mission education classes, by reading and learning all she could about followers of Islam. She had made significant friendships among several African foreign students. But scuba diving! What else could I find that seemed to be life-giving to her and yet would be of value to the kingdom of God? In preparation for our next appointment I reflected on some rather disconnected thoughts and ideas based upon our last conversation: scuba-diving instructor—Africa—a heart for Muslims. Then a light began to dawn! Might there be a place in Africa, especially in a country with restricted access, where a scuba diving instructor could serve, a place with a developing tourist industry, a hotel or travel agency waiting to introduce vacationers to the beauty and adventure of exploring tropical fish–filled coral reefs?

I made a few calls, followed up a few contacts, and did a lot of praying. When Jan came for her next appointment, I was ready. I shared with her some creative ideas for fulfilling her passion for ministry. She would only need to redirect her recreational hobby into a vocational opportunity at a tourist hotel I had located in the Comoros Islands, a Muslim country off the coast of Africa. This hotel needed a licensed scuba diving instructor. I had found an evangelical mission that would provide her with pastoral support in the field.

I would have totally failed her if I had tried to fit her into *my* plan. But God did have a wonderful plan awaiting her. In working together to identify her own dreams and desires, to discover that special gift in her hand, we created an opportunity for service that fulfilled all her dreams!

Beware of Lone Rangers

Christian vocational decisions should not be made in isolation. A calling is best clarified when affirmed by those who know the individual best. Then the call is informed by the individual's lifestyle and ministry habits. Mission pastors and vocational guidance counselors have interviewed eager mission volunteer applicants who can easily explain what they want to do and where they want to go, but their explanation is totally disconnected from their vocational or ministry involvements. "I want to go on a mission assignment to someplace in Africa. I think God is calling me." But the inquirer has made no effort to discover ministry in the African-American community at his doorstep! A burden for people in the Philippines makes little sense in the life of one who has made absolutely no effort to develop friendships among Filipino Americans in his own city. There is a threefold validation test helpful in discerning a person's professed call:

1. What is the *objective* evidence? Listen for the interviewee to say, "This is what I am currently *doing.*"
2. What is the *subjective* evidence that helps support this objective decision? ("This is how I am *feeling.*")
3. What is the *collective* evidence? ("This is what others are *saying* concerning my decision.")

Take the time necessary to help inquirers validate their call, then begin the guidance process to help those persons make more informed decisions regarding career choice and mission assignment. These three sources of evidence help determine an individual's *vision.* When vision is clarified, we can guide inquirers in the choice of *vehicle*: What mission agency can they best serve under and what field partner seems to be most appropriate? Guiding inquirers through the critical choice of an agency to serve with will help them match their vision, interest, and skills. Matching their theological understandings and cultural preferences to an appropriate agency and location is very important. When *vision* is clarified and the sending *vehicle* is determined, then the ministry *venue* for those persons can be determined after they arrive in the location of the desired ministry.

An Endless Variety of Service Opportunities

Midge was a product of the sixties, still clothed in the persona of an alternative lifestyle. But she had a strong personal commitment to Jesus Christ. She was a highly intelligent person with well-developed writing skills. She spoke both Hebrew and Arabic. For some reason known only to her, Midge had a strong interest in China, especially its remote tribal groups. With her orientation to simple living and with a disciplined mind skilled in research, Midge found her very special second career living in Hong Kong and traveling to the most remote corners of China and Tibet for the purpose of doing research on unreached people groups. She authored or edited several books on the minority groups in China who are most unreached with the gospel. One of Midge's books was used by conference attendees at Lausanne II who were interested in evangelizing these minority groups.

Mike was a commercial printer and active member of our mission department. He had a special interest in Muslims and often wondered how he might use his vocational skills in serving this group of people. While Mike was quite interested in a mission assignment, his wife felt keenly the responsibilities of rearing their two children and did not feel comfortable considering a volunteer mission experience in a distant and perhaps dangerous country. As Mike kept his sense of missionary challenge before her, one day Donelyn responded, "Well, if you can find a missionary assignment in England, then I am willing to go!" Donelyn knew that her commitment was a safe one. No one ends up assigned to missionary service in England! Not long afterward while Mike and I were exploring his ministry dreams, I shared with him an opportunity that had just come to my attention. A mission agency that provides Christian literature for the Muslim world needed a printer with the skills to typeset by computer in order to translate and publish their material in Arabic. Mike was both eager and guarded in his response. He said he was willing to go anywhere, but jokingly related to me that his wife's call was limited to England. I couldn't believe what he told me. The printer that was needed to fill this job would be located in southern England! Soon after, the entire family left for their field assignment and served effectively for several years until the translation and publication task was completed. God really is interested in finding that special place of service that fulfills the desires of our heart!

Viola's career had been in personnel and office administration. Now in retirement she came to share her interest in a cross-cultural service opportunity. After hearing about her vocational accomplishments and knowing of her giftedness for administrative detail, I could see that Viola was open to a variety of mission opportunities tailored to her skills. It did not take long to find that first special posting. Viola began in India, serving in a mission to the sightless disabled. From there she moved to Ecuador, where she served Wycliffe Bible Translators as a temporary office manager. After returning from these assignments she found life in Seattle a bit boring! Soon she was off on a new assignment as office coordinator for the Albania Encouragement Project in Albania's capital city of Tirana. She continues to volunteer in the mission office of the Presbyterian Church (U.S.A.), coordinating short-term service assignments and administratively supporting missionaries serving abroad.

Discovering your vocation could cost you your life! In an earlier generation a young Scotsman, Peter Cameron Scott, left his village to train for a safe and traditional ministry in London. Through his reading and various personal contacts he developed a passion to minister to unreached tribal people dwelling in the remote inland areas of Africa. Upon completion of his ministerial training, he set out for Africa. After only a short time of ministry, he was afflicted with malaria and almost died. Friends, despairing for his life, encouraged him to return home in order to recuperate. He followed their advice and regained his health. When he returned to West Africa he invited his brother John to accompany him. They were not many months in the field when Peter was afflicted with a tropical illness again. His brother John, despairing for his life, prevailed upon him to return home again to recuperate. During his long months of convalescence, Peter one day visited Westminster Abbey. As he walked down the central aisle of the nave he noticed a marble slab in the floor, which marked the final resting place of David Livingstone, England's first Protestant missionary to the wilds of Africa. His heart was strangely moved by the words from John 10:16 etched upon the face of the monument: "Other sheep have I who are not of this fold; they too will hear and follow me."

The flame of passion that had burned so brightly in the young and willing heart of Peter Cameron Scott was reignited once again. He found further inspiration in the apostle Paul's words: "Christ will be exalted in my body, whether by life or by death" (Philippians 1:20). After only a few more weeks of recuperating, Peter was off again for a third and final missionary journey to his beloved tribal people in Africa. In just a few short months, however, illness snuffed out his fragile life. Yet, here was one young man who discovered his special call, one young man who invested his resources to live out his passion, one young man empowered by the Holy Spirit who exchanged his life for the life of others. From his selfless example and leadership, the Africa Inland Mission was born. Jim Elliott, Wheaton College graduate of the fifties, knew what he spoke of when he wrote in his spiritual journal, "He is no fool to give up what he cannot keep in exchange for what he cannot lose."

Within the context of these examples, and with the burning passion of divine call, I have seen so many laymen and laywomen respond to God's call to cross-cultural ministry. A theology of vocation will assist one in finding God's special place of service and will enable leaders in any church to successfully guide mission inquirers into fruitful kingdom service.

4

Recruiting or Releasing?
The Empowerment of Laity

*T*here was a knock on my study door. Upon answering it I met a woman who introduced herself as Barbara. She was a member of our congregation that I had never met. I asked how I could assist her.

"I came to inquire about the recruitment announcement that was in last Sunday's worship service bulletin."

Knowing that I had placed five different announcements in that bulletin, I asked her which of the five had caught her attention.

"I want to talk to you about the one that suggested a free vacation on white sandy beaches!" she replied. I could see that she was amused with the announcement but seriously interested in the ministry opportunity the announcement described.

I believe in proactive recruiting, not merely reacting to others' requests. In recruiting, my focus is always upon the inquirer's gifts and skills rather than just on the needs and opportunities mission agencies publish. I try to visualize those members who will read these announcements I am preparing. What are their gifts and skills? What are their dreams for ministry? How do they understand God's call? How can I present them with opportunities for service that are compelling and that match their vocational skills? In promoting mission opportunities I try to keep in mind the ministry interests of the church member rather than the personnel needs of any particular mission society. Our congregation is filled with gifted professionals: public school teachers and university faculty members, lawyers, physicians, nurses and other health practitioners, accountants, financial planners, and stockbrokers. It is so important to know who your people are when you plan a recruiting strategy. Presenting opportunities for service that bear little relationship to your members' work experiences tends to be self-defeating. It only perpetuates the feeling that mission is always something that concerns others more than it does me!

I knew very well what Barbara meant when she told me she was interested in the announcement about the white sandy beaches. This announcement had read:

> Would you like to have an all-expense-paid vacation on the white sandy beaches of the Indian Ocean? Needed: A volunteer accountant, preferably with CPA credentials, willing to commit for a one- to two-year term of service in Mozambique. Project audit experience needed. Helpful if the inquirer is single and speaks Portuguese. Contact the Office of Urban and Global Mission.

I encouraged Barbara to share her story with me. Amazingly, her background matched wonderfully the needs mentioned in the announcement. Barbara said she had recently sold her business, a private accounting firm. Barbara herself was an accountant and had impressive contract audit experience. Most of her clients had been nonprofit organizations.

World Vision had requested that I recruit an auditor/ financial manager for this position. Their need was urgent. (I encourage several mission agencies and parachurch ministries to inform me of their "hot lists" of personnel needed for various mission projects.) In promoting these staff needs I prioritize those that seem to fit best the professional skills and vocational experiences of our congregation. World Vision was confronted with a serious crisis in its office in Mozambique. This office was responsible for administering a large-scale relief effort, but needed an accountant immediately. Barbara possessed those exact skills needed for this task! In expressing her interest, she indicated that she was ready to go anywhere, but Africa seemed to hold a special attraction for her. Best of all, she was single and ready to go!

"However, I need to tell you that my father had two wives."

With no context for the statement, I presumed that Barbara had decided that mission service was reserved only for those from perfect families, and that anything less than family perfection would disqualify even the most prepared for mission service. But I needed to understand her statement in order to give her good counsel.

"My father was first married to my mother."

Nothing unusual here, I concluded.

"When my mother died my father married my mother's sister. Oh yes, and I need to tell you that both of them were from Brazil and I grew up speaking Portuguese!"

How could I have ever known? In advertising for a Portuguese-speaking recruit, I had very minimal expectations that I would find anyone with this background. But at least it alerted potential applicants to the possibility of foreign language requirements!

This experience demonstrated that creativity in writing bulletin announcements was beginning to pay off. Most bulletin announcements are so uninterestingly written that they are of little interest to the reader. But offering an all-expense-paid vacation has interest even for the most disinterested pew warmer!

This is only the beginning of Barbara's story. Not long after her initial visit, World Vision appointed Barbara to a one-year term in Mozambique. An auditor and financial manager with her impressive credentials and experience could clear up the problem within this reasonable time frame. She completed her responsibilities ably and on time but remained in Mozambique for another eight years, serving with several different Christian organizations. She invested much of her personal time in the street boys of Maputo, Mozambique's run-down and impoverished capital city. These boys were not so much runaways as throwaways. Their fathers had been killed in the war or had deserted their families because of the horrible social disruptions of the war. Mothers could no longer afford to place food on the table for all their children. Often the eldest son, usually a preteen boy, was sent out of the home to fend for himself on the streets. There just wasn't enough food for all! Educational opportunities for these young boys ceased. They were often forced by their circumstances to lead a life of petty street crime. Barbara was concerned for these boys, both for their spiritual and their socioeconomic needs. Joined by other expatriate volunteers, she started a soap factory that provided these boys an honorable way to earn income. They no longer needed to support themselves by picking pockets, shoplifting, and engaging in other street crimes. This income became the means for restoring these boys to their homes and families. To think that this all began with a simple but creative announcement: "Would you like to have an all-expense-paid vacation on the white sandy beaches of the Indian Ocean?"

Recruiting or Releasing?

Early in my ministry I expended a great deal of effort in attempting to recruit people for leadership or service ministry roles: "I need three Sunday school teachers, four ushers, a youth advisor, and a lay preacher for our church's monthly service at Union Gospel Mission. God *needs* you! The church *needs* you! I *need* you! You *need* to become involved." Often those who did respond to this appeal were already overinvolved in the church's activities. I was able to recruit some of the volunteers needed. But it was quite another matter to keep these volunteers motivated and committed to their tasks for the necessary length of time. Some became weary long before their tasks were completed. With my persuasive skills I had encouraged them to do something that was neither life-giving nor appropriate to their personal set of skills, talents, and interests. They were just trying to be faithful—to fill needs that others defined. There is a big difference between recruiting people for ministry others have defined and releasing people for ministries that they have created or discovered!

God desires to see laypersons involved in witness and service; his desire is far greater than ours. The Holy Spirit is a very effective recruitment officer. The Spirit can be trusted to both convict people of their need to serve and then empower them to succeed in fulfilling their God-given task. How freeing it is to give up personal responsibility for playing God in others' lives! It is far better to trust God to do the recruiting. When my personal skills of persuasion become the determining factor in eliciting a positive response from a volunteer and if that ministry assignment does not turn out positively, the tendency is for the volunteer to blame the recruiter for the resulting negative feelings: "Maybe I shouldn't have been so easily persuaded to take this volunteer assignment. Perhaps I was talked into doing something that just isn't right for me!" I am slowly learning that it is better to be a birth attendant for another person's idea or dream than to be a dynamic visionary persuader, out to recruit volunteers to follow my dream.

Pastor Bruce Larson half jokingly exclaimed in a Sunday morning sermon, "My dream is to see a thousand UPC members serving in cross-cultural mission on any Sunday morning, with the remaining members here at home providing support to those who have gone. This way we can solve our parking problem!" Bruce is the last person to try and recruit others to share his dreams. Quite the opposite. He successfully created a congregational culture of risk-taking. Congregational members were encouraged to take a risk in following God's call for service. All were encouraged to grow daily in their faith journey. Part of that growth included discovering ministry opportunities reaching beyond anything heretofore imagined. These ministries were important for the kingdom of God and became life-giving and life-changing for the volunteers involved.

Ray and Sandra were an active mission-minded couple. Ray was trained as a nautical engineer. Sandra was employed by the Seattle park district. Over the years they had volunteered for many ministries as a part of their regular church life. They also served as members of our mission department and enthusiastically participated in church-centered mission activities and mission education classes. They provided leadership for our biweekly Mission Preparation Fellowship. One day they shared with me their dissatisfaction with their current careers and expressed their growing interest in volunteering for a cross-cultural ministry opportunity. Ray had just returned from a short-term mission in Haiti. This had turned his world upside down. But Sandra was not so sure that what had turned Ray on spiritually was really what she desired. We met together often for discussion and prayer. One day Sandra expressed a readiness to take her own risk! She signed up for a short-term mission experience independent of Ray. Somewhere during her time in Haiti she saw what God saw! When Sandra returned, she and Ray discovered that they now shared a genuine desire to return to Haiti for longer-term service. They gave their employers notice, enlisted a few young singles to rent their two homes, and then developed their financial and spiritual support team. Following their prefield preparation and training they departed for Port-au-Prince for a one-year term. That was twelve years ago! There have been many changes in field work assignments and an abundance of personal struggles and ministry difficulties, but they remain deeply committed to the people of Haiti, ministering to both their spiritual and physical needs. Through their commitment—their willingness to take a personal risk—they continue to serve as both model and mentor to many others in the process of discovering their own ministry challenge.

Creating a User-Friendly Environment

The responsibility of a mission leader is to release people to those ministries that God places in their hearts. It is not to recruit people for ministry slots other people desire to see filled. A primary task for every pastor or lay leader is to develop those strategies that will be most effective in releasing people for those ministries that excite and challenge them.

Marta served Seattle Pacific University as chaplain and organizer of student-led short-term mission trips. While accompanying these teams she developed a personal interest in African people and ministry. One summer she visited Ghana and Kenya to gather information for her doctoral studies. She researched the similarities and differences between African and American student spirituality. Marta returned from this assignment and told me that, while she was perfectly content with her professional work at the university, if I ever found something challenging for her to do in Africa, I was to let her know. Now that's a challenge I can't resist! Later I shared Marta's interest with the director of Nairobi's Daystar University. He was impressed with my description of Marta's spiritual gifts and cross-cultural sensitivity and encouraged Marta to write him concerning her interests. Soon after, Marta was commissioned for a missionary task ideally suited to both her interests and the university's needs. Marta was released for a ministry perfectly suited for her rather than recruited for a position that might best suit another. Her one-year commitment continues now in a long-term assignment. Marta has been blessed by the experience, and the students at Daystar University have profited from her special skills and insights. In addition, she has adopted two Kenyan children. Her life and ministry now are deeply rooted in Kenyan soil.

Developing That
"Every Member a Minister" Mentality

Congregations that accomplish great things for the kingdom of God are of no single denomination or theological heritage. What they share is their commitment to lay mobilization. Christ Church in Bristol, England; Capitol City Baptist Church in Quezon City, Philippines; Young Nak Presbyterian Church in Seoul, Korea; and the large Assembly of God Church on Park Avenue in Calcutta, India, all share something very important in common. They are fully committed and totally mobilized to recruit, train, and deploy their laity in ministry. These lay ministers contribute their talents and skills to build the local congregation and to engage in evangelistic and church-planting ministries. They provide amazing social ministries that change the face of their communities. In Calcutta I have participated with scores of men and women who arise long before daybreak every morning. The women labor tirelessly in the church kitchens, preparing food for the thirty-two thousand women and children who receive a nourishing hot meal each day. The men load the food and drive the trucks. They deliver these meals to nearby slums and distant villages daily. And these lay ministers offer homeless thousands the bread of life even as they share physical bread. Capitol City Baptist Church and Young Nak Presbyterian Church have sent their volunteers in mission to the unreached peoples in their own countries, and to mission service in many countries overseas. Christ Church of Bristol has provided the Anglican Church in England with a whole new model for lay-led ministries. Each of these congregations knows its purpose will be fulfilled best through their men and women claiming their rights as "a chosen people, a royal priesthood" (1 Peter 2:9).

Caring . . . Shaping . . . Giving . . . Going!

I was a bit disappointed when we changed our church logo. It probably needed a redesign, but I think its message lost some of the punch it was designed to convey. It bore just four simple words: "Caring . . . Shaping . . . Giving . . . Going!" These four words powerfully express how ministry develops. While our size and program at University Presbyterian Church identify us as a *megachurch,* we work hard to create a congregational culture of a small church. We create as many entry points to the church and its various ministries as possible. We design support groups for every need and initiate programs and encourage relationships that minister to every conceivable need, interest, and skill. We encourage every member to become involved in a small group. We work hard at becoming clusters of *caring* communities sharing ministry with one another. The *shaping* is first the work of the Holy Spirit. Leadership's responsibility is to "equip the saints for the work of ministry, for building up the body of Christ" (Ephesians 4:12). When these needs are met, people are ready to respond to the *giving* aspect of ministry. They will invest their time, talent, and resources in ministries that they have been a part of creating and shaping. In these small groups and ministry teams the lay ministers keep accountable to God and to one another. *Going* becomes an almost automatic response to the service culture and the risk-taking environment we have created. And it works! They go out by the hundreds to discover their own unique ministry opportunities. They accept gladly their ministry responsibilities and serve with enthusiasm.

Ordaining Pastors and Commissioning Priests

Our congregation's pastors are discouraged from taking leadership roles in initiating new ministries. In order to encourage lay ownership, we strive to have ministry initiatives begin with the laity. It was to a simple Galilean fisherman that Jesus first delivered his most powerful promise to the church: "I will build my church, and the gates of Hades will not overcome it" (Matthew 16:18). This same lay apostle understood the church as a "chosen people, a royal priesthood, a holy nation, a people belonging to God" (1 Peter 2:9).

At the Lausanne II Congress in Manila I met Lee Yih, a successful Hong Kong business entrepreneur. He was one of the more popular speakers at the conference and made an interesting analogy of frogs and lizards that was intended to give listeners a clearer understanding of the importance of lay mobilization for mission service and witness. He humorously noted the differences between frogs (the clergy) and lizards (the laity), by noting the eating habits of these reptiles:

> Frogs sit and wait until their prey walks, flies, or swims past—and then they pounce. Everything comes to him who waits in the frog world. Lizards, however, would die if they sat and waited. They go out in search of food. This is how the church goes about its business. Vocational workers normally have their work brought to them. If they are going to preach the gospel, a church or hall is booked in which they stand to speak. Other people drag in the populace. Others bring the ministry to them. The lizards—lay persons—go out to their daily occupations; they meet the general public in the form of their neighbors, friends, and workmates, fellow club members in the normal course of their lives. The frogs—pastors—are too often isolated from real people. Indeed, real people are often frightened of them, and avoid them. . . . In the case of particularly big frogs, they hide away in hotel rooms to avoid contact much of the time, whereas lizards are unthreatening, and always there, ready to take the opportunity to talk about Christ when offered. This is real full-time Christian service!

The crowd responded with loud applause and a standing ovation. The need for a highly mobilized laity was a truth embraced by all. Effective means to fill that need are much slower in coming. One of life's greatest rewards is to help others release their skills, giftedness, and resources, and to see this giftedness channeled into ministry inspired and led by lay people. Lay ministers are often at the forefront of mission outreach today. They spread out across the face of the earth and bear witness to God's kingdom. The church of Jesus Christ needs all of the priests and all of the pastors its forces can muster in order to accomplish this challenging but vital task of world evangelization!

5

Mission Is Better
Caught Than Taught

Investing More While Reaping Less

I often consult with church mission committees
who wish to increase their congregation's involvement in missions. When invited to preach for Sunday services, I agree with one stipulation. Either on
Saturday night or following the services on Sunday,
I want the opportunity to meet for a couple of hours
with the congregation's governing body, its pastor
and staff, and its mission and stewardship leaders.
This gives me the opportunity to challenge leadership to consider how they might mobilize more
resources for congregation-based mission outreach.
I ask specific questions so I can understand their
strategy for congregational mission promotion. Typ-
ically, the annual mission conference is often singled
out as their most important tool to inspire laity and
promote their various mission causes. When this is
their answer I share with them the three responses I
most often hear from those who evaluate their
annual conference: (1) "This has been the most challenging and exciting mission conference we've ever
sponsored here in our church!" (2) "Wow! Are we
exhausted! I'm not sure I want to volunteer for this
activity next year," and (3) "We're really disappointed!

This year's conference was our very best effort but it is so disappointing that so few people attended!"

Does this sound a bit familiar? This is why I keep asking the same question: "Why is it that you invest your greatest efforts in the one mission activity that seems to produce the least results?" Though some conferences are especially effective in smaller churches, many times in larger churches with more regular program opportunities fewer positive results are gleaned from the effort. There are so many program options to choose from, unless one is highly motivated for mission, one will usually skip the mission conference in favor of becoming directly involved in other church activities that are tailored to more clearly meet personal interests and needs. We soon discover that the increased energy, creativity, and resources expended seem to impact a smaller percentage of the membership each year.

Creatively Capturing
Attention for Mission

An effective means for developing mission interest is available every Sunday in regular worship services. In addition to all of the usual components of a Reformed worship service, we prioritize time for lay witness. Each week an individual (or sometimes a married couple) is carefully selected by the pastoral team to share with the congregation some meaningful life experience. The "witness," in the format of an interview, is always a very personal story and sometimes that experience will relate to the sermon topic of the day. But whether related to the sermon or not, the person and the basic theme of the story are selected for their relevance to all that is planned for that worship service. One of our pastors takes responsibility for conducting the interview. It is important that the person is well prepared in telling his story so that it keeps on track. The interviewing pastor works with the person sharing the witness during the week preceding the worship services to help the individual focus his story. There is a simple, standard format of questions we use in preparing to tell the story: How did Christ become real in your life? How is God actively involved in your life today? What have you learned that might be helpful to your brothers and sisters in the congregation? These are simple but direct questions, and they help persons clearly communicate what they want to say and maintain the focus of their witness. The interviewer and interviewee must fit questions and answers into the four- to five-minute time slot allotted. If it doesn't fit, the interviewer will surely hear about it at next week's staff meeting!

This lay witness is not for the purpose of promoting church programs. It is all about how that individual experiences Christ in daily life, how some life experience has resulted in greater spiritual growth, how God has met that person in a very painful or difficult life experience. On a regular basis, members who are either going out on mission or freshly returning from a ministry outreach are chosen as the witnesses. This is planned, not to give them an opportunity to relate all of their mission experiences and challenges, but rather to let them select something from the experience that has been life-changing or has given them a much deeper understanding of God. This is one of our most effective means to communicate mission. Think of the average Joe in your congregation. Up until this point in the worship service, Joe may not be fully involved in the worship experience—more a spectator than a participant. Then Joe's best friend, John, is introduced as today's witness! You can be sure that at this point Joe's listening interest has increased several times! As John shares how Christ became real in his life, Joe is able to relate to his friend's experiences as similar to his own. As John tells of his professional life as an engineer, he relates to the congregation how he has just returned from a Middle Eastern country where for six months he worked as an engineering consultant. Out of his loneliness, he found a very small community of Christians where he could make friends. "Christians there are a very persecuted minority," he shares. "I found them so ready to receive encouragement and support from me. I suddenly realized that while I had gone out as an engineer, God was giving me an opportunity to serve them as a missionary! I discovered new ways where I could minister while I learned so much from their faithfulness to Christ while living with adversity." I suggest that any person traveling overseas on a work assignment find ways that they can encourage local believers and perhaps have the opportunity to share appropriately their Christian faith with others. Whether they share their story to one person or to a congregation, it will be a powerful experience for both the storyteller and for the listener.

By the end of his story, you can be certain that John's very personal witness has captured the interest of many folks in the congregation. Through hearing John's experience, Joe, for the first time in his life, begins to discover how ministry can become a part of his regular work and family life. And Joe realizes that mission just might have something to do with him: "This is amazing! If my friend John can be a missionary, then *anybody* can become one, and that anybody might even include me!" Whether Joe's mission interest is ignited by a personal mission experience or by another layperson's shared experience does not really matter. Inviting individuals familiar with the congregation to share their experiences communicates mission more powerfully than many of the more traditional times we set aside for a "Moment for Mission." However, the impact of mission witness will be diminished if it becomes a routine part of the worship experience. The mission story should be just one of the lay witnesses given, perhaps four to eight per year.

A Mission-Minded Church Is a Church with Mission on Its Mind

Leaders must make mission interest and involvement accessible to all. Surround and saturate the congregation with information, reports, personal witness, and consciousness-raising reminders that will assist every member to *think* mission. Mission should be as normal as breathing out and breathing in! On the day Jesus returned to his Father, he placed mission at the very center of church life: "You will receive power when the Holy Spirit has come upon you; and you will be my witnesses in Jerusalem, in all Judea and Samaria, and to the ends of the earth" (Acts 1:8). As we learn to speak the language of the laity, to develop effective mission communication and education strategies that reflect their needs and interests, we will feel enormous creative mission energy in our congregations.

Mission awareness is better *caught* than *taught*! Surround your congregation with opportunities for mission challenge. We use all the creative input possible from every sector of our congregation's life to keep mission in the forefront of our interests and activities. Here are a few ideas and techniques we have found most helpful in promoting general mission education all year long:

> • Classified ads in our worship bulletin that offer available mission service opportunities consistent with the skills and experiences of our laity and compatible and consistent with our mission focus.

- Picture boards, maps, and other materials that support the activities of our missionaries and mission projects. We change these frequently and make them visually attractive (lots of pictures and graphics, fewer words!). These need to be contemporary in style and action oriented. Provide some type of response device to enable viewers to respond to the appeal.
- Planned space in the church newsletter for missionaries to share their stories rather than to promote their projects.
- A host/hostess at the coffee hour who can provide members an opportunity for introduction and informal contact with the church's missionaries during a visit to the congregation.
- A special booth in the church's narthex where international guests can register and then meet interested friends.
- Mission volunteers or career missionaries who can share their experiences with the various interest groups already scheduled in your church program rather than to new classes that appeal only to mission-mobilized members.

General Mission Education

While it is true that many churches place unrealistic expectations on mission conferences that attract a small minority of church members, traditional mission conferences can be an effective means of introducing mission to the noninvolved members. It can provide time and program space in an overloaded church calendar. Prioritize a weekend or a full week when mission becomes the central focus of congregational life. Keep the planned activities and the message tightly focused on the goals you wish to achieve both in your mission conference and your ongoing mission program. The more focused the conference, the more effective it will be in communicating the vision and bringing the results you wish to achieve. About every third or fourth year we have used the all-church mission emphasis or conference as a means to involve more members in understanding the congregation's mission outreach. We try always to design ways that will challenge them toward personal involvement. Here are a few ideas that have been helpful for us:

1. From the beginning, empower a group of lay leaders to take responsibility for planning the conference. Include those volunteers whose skills and experience will support the committee when moving from planning to program implementation.

2. Develop a clear focus for the event that will undergird your current missions and missionaries, while challenging the participants to new mission outreach.

3. Select presenters and resource persons who will most effectively communicate mission. A successful speaker at an Urbana Conference is not necessarily the one who will reach your congregation. Select speakers who know your mission philosophy and the congregation's culture. People need to hear mission challenge in a language and style consistent with their culture, not a mission-minded subculture.

4. Plan the public events in the time periods most convenient for those you wish to attract to the conference. Fewer events more highly focused and presented at times more friendly to laypeople's schedules will go a long way in making your conference successful.

5. Make sure that your conference will be more than a "listening event." Set up "*chat rooms*" to give participants opportunities to discuss with resource persons and other members what they are hearing and to express how they are feeling about what they hear.

6. Invite as participants any local mission agencies that are consistent with your mission outreach and program

focus. They will then have the opportunity to recruit volunteers for various ministries and answer interested inquirers' questions.

7. Invite other local congregations who share common interests to be a part of the event. Smaller churches can sponsor much larger and more interesting conferences by sharing the resources of others. Larger congregations can include smaller churches in order to provide mission experiences in a shared conference that these smaller churches could never afford by themselves.

8. Mobilize! Mobilize! Mobilize! A mission conference that shares only information but provides no practical opportunities for involvement will have little lasting value for those attending. The conference needs to move participants from listening to acting in any or all of the following ways:

- mobilize prayer resources so that prayer might undergird all of your mission programs and missionaries;
- mobilize lay volunteers for local and global mission involvement;
- mobilize financial resources to undergird missions and missionaries;
- mobilize skill resources by helping lay participants identify those personal skills that will support your planned mission activities.

9. Be sure to evaluate the conference soon after its conclusion so that you might preserve what was most effective and identify what was not. It is surprising how quickly we forget these things. Honest and timely evaluation will help you in planning a more effective event next time.

Sharing the News

Several years ago we began shifting our mission emphasis toward more involvement in local mission. We

were much stronger in our global outreach than we were
in developing new and innovative programs for our urban
setting. The mission conference we planned that year
helped move us toward that goal. We never had a short-
age of lay volunteers for service abroad, but we needed to
see more of them become mission volunteers in our city.
Thus, the recruitment of urban mission volunteers was set
as the goal for the conference. Dr. Raymond Bakke, mission professor at Northern Baptist Seminary and experienced urbanologist, was invited as our resource person
and plenary speaker. "Christ for the Cities" was selected
as the conference's theme. We had never sponsored an
urban mission event before. Here are some of the things
we planned that helped us move toward a heightened
interest and involvement in urban mission:

1. We invited a large downtown church to serve as
cosponsor of the conference. This church struggled to
maintain its vital ministry in a rapidly changing community. Membership had declined rapidly during the last
decade. Members were overwhelmed by the problems of
the inner city and had lost some of their skills in communicating effectively to a changing urban population. By
partnering with them we were able to share both our
strengths and weaknesses. By planning the event in their
location we were able to understand the city from a different perspective. They experienced our request to partner with them in the conference as a sign of support and
encouragement.

2. We invited other area churches who shared a commitment to the gospel and a concern for mission in the
city. Participants were registered from fifty-seven congregations in the all-day urban seminars!

3. We recruited those community ministry organizations
that needed more of our congregations' human and financial resources to accomplish their mission. They were

encouraged by our interest and successfully recruited many new volunteer workers for their ministries. We profited from their experience and professional expertise.

Whatever means you create to raise mission consciousness, always remember that most important ideas are better *caught* than *taught*. Mission is surely one of those great ideas! We can spend too much time and energy teaching mission theory and not enough time demonstrating mission and recruiting mission volunteers. Church members are always looking for the information and experiences that best fit into their busy lives.

6

The Making of World Christians

*A*part from the general mission education provided for the entire congregation, there are areas of more specialized mission education and training needed by lay members with more highly focused mission interest. These same educational opportunities can encourage others who are on the periphery of mission interest but seem ready to advance further in mission interest and knowledge. We have developed two basic study tracks to meet this training need. This course is similar to "Perspectives on the World Christian Movement" that was developed by the U.S. Center for World Mission. It has been very effective in introducing mission to the uninitiated and in providing further training in mission history, philosophy, and policies for effective mission engagement.

Because we needed to adapt this course to our more specific congregational needs, we redesigned it to become part of our "Becomers" series. At first, this series consisted of three classes. "Becoming Christian" is designed to encourage a person's journey to faith. In this class the inquirer is introduced to the essential tenets of the Christian faith and is challenged to begin that important personal faith journey. "Becoming the Church" is our new members' preparation class. Here prospective members learn the basics of our congregation's life and witness. During the class they are each placed in a small group and then encouraged to become members of a regular small group when the class is completed. Opportunities are given to encourage them to find specialized areas for their own service and witness. Additionally, this is the class where we help them develop their Christian stewardship understanding and responsibilities and discover how these are best fulfilled within the context of our church. The "Becoming a Minister" class equips laity for service. Spiritual gifts are examined and applied to personal life experiences. "Becoming a World Christian," our redesign of the "Perspectives on the World Christian Movement" course, became the fourth in the series of classes offered. The curriculum was designed to broaden and deepen one's understanding of the Great Commission and then to teach how to apply these principles for effective cross-cultural witness. Here are the major topics covered in the course:

- A Biblical Basis for Mission
- The Kingdom of God and Its Mission
- Contemporary Mission Challenges Understood within the Context of Mission History
- Emerging Trends in Mission Today
- How to Develop Cross-Cultural Understanding
- Biculturalism and Effective Cross-Cultural Communication
- Effective Strategies for Today's Mission Challenges
- The Face of the Poor and the Face of God: Evangelization and Social Concern
- Empowerment of People: Developing Strategic Mission Partnerships
- Mission Challenges and Ecumenical Commitments
- Skill Development for Dialogue and Discussion

This subject matter in no way comprehensively covers all that can be learned about mission, whether that learning is from the scripture, from history, or from the context of contemporary mission activity. But these lessons do provide students with an overview of the most strategic areas of learning and give them a starting place for further self-education and broader mission experience. Rather than just duplicating our "Becomers" series, each church whether small or large will know best how to design the type of instructional series that best meets its needs. "Becoming a World Christian" has been the catalyst for launching many of our lay members into short-term mission service. Some of these volunteers have remained for longer terms than they had originally planned. Brad and Wendy now serve with Wycliffe Bible Translators in South Asia, Walt and Laila pioneer mission in Albania, Sandra and Ray manage short-term mission teams in Haiti and Central America, Pam serves in Albania as a university student worker to develop a national student movement, then continues her ministry in a Central Asian republic where she is helping to establish a national InterVarsity movement. These persons first caught the vision in this class.

In 1997, Dr. William Taylor, director of the World Evangelical Fellowship's missions commission, invited me to join forty other world mission leaders in developing criteria for missionary education and training. We met together and in small groups for a full week, sharing our experiences, exchanging ideas, and identifying those qualities that we observed in the lives of missionaries whose ministries were most effective. Several training centers in Asia, Africa, and Latin America contributed to the development of these criteria. Those who were most affected by the mission or missionary activity were helpful in developing this list of indispensable qualities of ministry skills that should be required of missionary candidates. In the end the study group decided that effective missionary training programs will include the following elements, listed in order of priority:

1. Develop spiritual character.
2. Enhance skills in learning to live successfully in community.
3. Shape a personal perspective in mission theology and practice.
4. Learn how to evangelize cross-culturally and relationally.
5. Develop standards for measuring ministry effectiveness.

After reviewing many training models and materials, these were the five most important and indispensable qualities and skills we all felt should be required for every missionary candidate. All five of these training priorities can be developed effectively at the local church level. None of them begin with sophisticated mission theory or highly organized outreach strategies. They are considered important because they refer to missionary character development. They are focused on developing spiritually and emotionally healthy individuals. Until these qualities of character are developed, all other missiological theory and outreach strategies are insufficient for qualifying the type of missionary candidate needed in today's complex world. For this very reason it requires that every mission-minded congregation assume major responsibility for beginning the missionary training process in the candidate's home congregation. If the candidates never become professional cross-cultural missionaries far from home, they will be well prepared to minister to the cross-cultural challenges of their own area. Missionary training modules must begin with the development of the whole person. The local church is uniquely qualified to accomplish this task.

Creative Curriculum Planning

To provide more specialized training opportunities for some of our urban mission volunteers, we developed other classes to prepare them for more effective mission service in their own communities. We developed a ten-week course offered at the same time our preaching series was based on the city. We entitled it "A Tale of Two Cities: The City of God and the Cities of Humankind—City Issues Examined and Answers Explored." This class's topics included:

- The Church in the City—Learning to Love the City!
- Poverty and Hunger—Ministry among the Poor That Reflects Christian Values
- No Vacancy—Friendships with the Forgotten Homeless
- Turf Troubles! New Names for Gang Youth
- Crime and Punishment—Ministering to the Imprisoned
- The Disintegration of the Urban Family
- Welcoming Ministries for Refugee Populations
- Racism and Reconciliation—Healing the Wounds of the Past
- Personal Faith and Public Witness

There are no limits to the variety of study courses any congregation can develop that will help prepare it for urban and global mission. To help foster creative thinking in your situation, here is another series of ten lessons. In this series we attempted to identify some contemporary mission challenges and to provide both learning and assistance to individuals interested in making a personal inventory of needs, talents, and opportunities for ministry. The class, "Preparing for a Life of Service in the 21st Century," was designed to prepare students to become kingdom people serving in a world of dramatic change. Topics included:

- How to Be Good News in a World of Pain
- Spiritual Survival Skills in a Hostile World
- Discover Your Key Motivational Themes
- Learn to Live with the City in Your Heart
- Strategic Engagement in a World of Disintegration
- Face Up to Your Cultural Challenges
- God So Loved . . . Whom?
- New Mission Frontiers in a New Century
- Learn to Live in Grace Cross-Culturally
- New Opportunities for a New Century of Service

The opportunities for creative curriculum design are endless. Here are some of the individual classes we developed to meet a specific need at a particular time:

- What the World Needs Now Is Love Sweet Love—The Ministry of Reconciliation in a World Filled with Religious and Ethnic Rivalries
- Does Africa Have a Future? What Is Africa's Challenge for Us?
- Proactive Believing—Signs and Wonders as Christian Witness
- America's Obsession with Power—The Use and Misuse of Giftedness
- Contemporary Challenges Facing the Church—Beyond Acts 28

Allow your creativity to run loose! Identify and engage those people in your congregation or community who can become effective teaching resources. Employ their skills and experiences to complement and broaden the church's educational offerings. There are far more potential teachers among your church members than even the largest church can employ, and these persons know much more clearly the specific needs of your congregation.

Mission Skill Training

General mission education is designed to communicate mission passion and to motivate lay people toward mission involvement. However, more comprehensive training and development needs to be available for those wishing to enter personal mission service. This training might take place in a group orientation class for those preparing for short-term mission service. Other opportunities can assist the missioner to develop more specific ministry skills. In these classes I try to include training in the following skills:

- Bible knowledge
- Bible study methods
- training in relational evangelism skills
- small group techniques
- the theology of mission
- cross-cultural living survival skills
- a maintenance schedule for spiritual wholeness
- prayer and spiritual warfare
- post–field service survival skills

Speak the Language of the People

Nonformal educational opportunities can often provide very effective skill preparation and development. In our "Language Acquisition for Mission Service" (LAMS) classes our goal is to motivate volunteers to begin language learning before they leave for their field assignment. LAMS also helps monitor language learning for those already serving in the field. This course was created by Carol Johnson, a member of our congregation who grew up as a missionary kid in Beirut, Lebanon. (She also developed our "Language Institute for Refugees," mentioned in chapter 8.) While a student at Fuller Seminary she became a teaching assistant to Tom and Betty Brewster. Here she learned the language-learning instructional method known as LAMP (Language Acquisition Made Practical). Thousands of new missionary recruits have benefited from employing these methods in their language-learning experience. This learning method requires total immersion in the culture of the people whose language is being learned, but the methods of learning can be taught at home. Carol has expanded our vision for what this type of instruction can accomplish. The LAMS class becomes a strong motivator for those traveling and working overseas to learn at least a small amount of the language where they will be living and working. It provides an opportunity to learn some simple phrases and market language related to the social interchange of the people where the candidate will serve. LAMS is available as a learning opportunity for any laypersons whose business assigns them oversees. With these language skills they have developed before leaving for the field, they can begin developing friendships as soon as they arrive. LAMS also provides a language-learning experience for lay volunteers who serve in various ethnic ministries in the local community. The process of cultural assimilation for ethnic minorities is accelerated when volunteers can speak their language.

Advance language learning is proactive preparation for mission service. Prepare your lay members now with some basic language-learning skills so that they will be more prepared to respond when God calls them to serve. They will be less fearful in responding. Fear of language learning often inhibits positive response. If your church does not have members who possess these language-teaching skills, then assess the possibilities in your community through the local community college or other institution or organization. Just a little language learning increases confidence and enhances cross-cultural adjustment.

City Dive—A Short-Term Urban Learning Experience

Many mission-learning experiences can be short in duration but long-lasting in ministry. And sometimes long-learning does *not* become long-lasting! Everything you plan will not necessarily succeed. It hasn't for us. But the old advice is good advice to follow when planning creative learning experiences: If at first you don't succeed, try, try again!

An urban mission intern created "City Dive" as a twenty-four-hour intensive learning experience that introduces lay members to life in the inner city. Few middle-class, suburban-dwelling individuals have experienced the unique ministry challenges in areas of the city where they neither reside nor work. City Dive is an active learning opportunity in which participants encounter urban issues and meet people who are the most underserved in our city. In this innovative learning experience, new ideas are developed, spiritual values are clarified, and personal growth is encouraged. Relationships begun on the streets become friendships that transform the volunteer and encourage the individual who feels isolated from the normal life in the city.

Our urban intern designed City Dive as an intensive weekend experience that makes it possible for most members to participate. The weekend includes volunteer service at inner-city missions, with special interest in serving the homeless and visiting low-income seniors and those needing specialized housing. In going on an outing, organizing an activity with homeless and disadvantaged children, or just walking the streets, participants become more familiar with the dynamics of street life and seek contact with homeless, disenfranchised, and hurting people. Participants spend Friday night in a safe inner-city mission setting. This experience includes an opportunity for prayer, biblical reflection, and writing. Spiritual journaling helps participants internalize their experience and see God at work in others. At the end of the weekend, participants gather for a debriefing so that they might share their experiences and stories while they are still fresh in their minds and hearts.

City Dive has been a way to immerse volunteers in city life so that they experience life from the underside. It helps them see the city with new eyes, and their hearts and minds become filled with a new understanding of God's intentions for the city and his special love for the poor. For many, it has become a life-changing experience. The unique pockets of need and pain in your city as well can become the catalyst for ministries that too often are considered only in some distant place.

In the task of creating world Christians in your congregation, you will need to plan both formal and nonformal mission education opportunities. To create the impression that only those with formal mission training are prepared for mission service will disenfranchise most of your congregation. To encourage untrained and unprepared members to engage in cross-cultural ministries both locally and globally, where cultural and communication issues are complex, will only bring discouragement, frustration, and failure. Unprepared missioners are perfect candidates for missionary burnout. Paul's words to the Ephesian Christians are especially relevant to cross-cultural ministers: God has given gifts to some as teachers "to prepare God's people for works of service, so that the body of Christ may be built up" (Ephesians 4:12).

7

Developing a Model
for Congregation-Based Mission

*M*ary caught my attention following the second morning worship service. "My son John and his wife are visiting this week from Lynn's home in England. John has asked me to see if you would be willing to meet with him." On further inquiry I discovered that John's interest in meeting was related to his interest in mission. Of course I agreed to the meeting! The Quanruds were members of our congregation. John spent some of his early school years here before heading off to Europe. While studying at a Bible institute in Sweden, John heard Dr. Peter Kuzmic, president of the Evangelical Theological Seminary in Yugoslavia, speak. Dr. Kuzmic shared his concerns for the spiritual needs of the people in the communist nations of Eastern Europe with the students. In a private conversation with Dr. Kuzmic following the chapel service, John asked if he could come to Osijek and enroll as a student in the seminary. Dr. Kuzmic encouraged John and Lynn to consider moving to Yugoslavia to become students at the university in Pristina, the capital of the Yugoslavian province of Kosovo. Here they could make friendships with Kosovar Albanians and begin to learn the Albanian language and culture. This could prepare them for any possible future ministry in Albania proper. Dr. Kuzmic shared his dream that some day, God is going to burst open the prison of that land and provide an opportunity for it to receive the good news of the gospel and that we need to begin preparing young men and women who will be ready for the task! John knew that since the end of World War II, Albania had been closed to the West and closed to Christianity and all other religions. After more than fifty years Albania remained the world's only constitutionally mandated atheistic nation.

My own interest in Albania began much earlier. In 1960 I had just completed my first year of missionary service in the Philippines when our mission's foreign secretary visited the field. This was the first time Dr. Edwin Jacques had visited me. I was eager to share with him all of our new ministry activities and opportunities. We spent every available minute talking about ministry in Manila. However, at supper the direction of the conversation changed. Dr. Jacques began reminiscing about his early years of missionary service. He and his wife Dorothy spent these years as missionaries to Albania. He was appointed for Albanian missionary service the same year I was born! Eight years later he, his wife, and children were the last American missionaries expelled from Albania by the Italian fascist government. This was just a few months before the onset of World War II. I still can remember the tears that moistened his cheeks as he recounted stories of those early missionary years. Dr. Jacques's deep love for the people of Albania was evident. This chance conversation became the beginning of my personal interest in Albania. I began to pray regularly for its people and government, that one day Albania would reopen for the preaching of the gospel.

John's time in my office brought back those memories of Dr. Jacques's affection for the Albanian people. I could see that John's concern and commitment was similar to Dr. Jacques's. John was certain of God's call to begin an

Albanian ministry now in Yugoslavia, while waiting for any future opportunity to go directly to Albania. "I am willing to wait for this even if I have to wait much of my life!" he asserted. He and Lynn were ready to begin ministry inside Albania the moment that a door opened, but in the meantime they would begin their Albanian ministry where they could. He wondered if his parents' home church would help provide financial support for their missionary undertaking. Dr. Jacques's, John's, and my concern for the Albanian people merged that day. Soon I shared this with our mission support committee, and they responded with enthusiasm and generosity: "This just may be our opportunity to do something in mission that God has been uniquely preparing us for!" Soon after, John and Lynn were commissioned as our missionaries to Albanians. While letters were exchanged and financial and prayer support continued, I had no opportunity to sit down again with John to share ideas and dreams until events overtook my plans to visit the Quanruds in Pristina. Since the collapse of the Berlin Wall, many felt it was only a matter of time until the government of Albania, the last bastion of Soviet-style Marxism, would collapse. That happened during the early days of February 1991. John and Lynn prepared to move to Albania immediately, but first revisited their home church for a time of planning and prayer.

Creating a Mission Laboratory

John and Lynn and their two children moved to Albania in June of that first year of Albania's democratic liberation. We helped them purchase a house in Albania's capital city of Tirana as their residence. A few months later I made my first of many visits to Albania. (Eight years later, I have just returned from my thirty-seventh visit!) Before they departed we agreed that while there they would concentrate their efforts on additional language learning and on building friendships with the Albanian people. They would keep us informed of the special opportunities to partner in ministry in this atheistic but traditionally Muslim country. Prior to World War II, 20 percent of Albanians were Orthodox Christians. Another 10 percent were Roman Catholic believers. There were about one hundred Protestant believers before the war, and only three of these were still alive in the summer of 1991. The incredible story of God's work in Albania during these past few years could fill several volumes. With the Quanruds now living in Albania, the congregation's interest in ministry there soared. We became an early and important part of the new evangelical witness. Through this Albanian ministry connection our entire mission program was transformed. We experienced congregational engagement in mission outreach in ways deemed impossible heretofore. With people movement hastened by jet travel and e-mail communications linking us to one another, our congregation's direct involvement in foreign mission outreach rose to new levels. We knew that there were no shortcuts to cultural immersion, language learning, building relationships, and developing visible presence, but we believed that these challenges could be met as we built an in-country mission team.

From this intensive immersion in Albanian ministry we have learned some of the principles that will help congregation-based mission service be effective. These are not absolutes as much as they are observations learned in the process of ministry.

Stop to See What God Has Been Doing before You Arrived

I sometimes get the idea that some missionaries act as though God hasn't arrived until they bring him with them in their suitcase! The psalmist reminds us that the whole creation already belongs to the Lord. The apostle Paul writes that God has made himself plain to all: "For since the creation of the world God's invisible qualities—his eternal power and divine nature—have been clearly seen, being understood from what has been made" (Romans 1:20). All men and women are without excuse before God because God is actively present in all countries and cultures. He is there before the missionary arrives and remains after the missionary leaves.

Before beginning ministry in a new location, stop to see what God has been doing before you arrived. Albania had suffered five centuries of oppression under the Ottoman Empire's control. During this time Christians and pagans were forcibly converted to Islam. These centuries were followed by fifty years of atheistic Marxism. Few remnants of Christianity remained. Muslim people and institutions suffered the same oppression. Albania's Orthodox and Roman Catholic churches had been either destroyed or confiscated. On the surface it could appear to newcomers that all Christian witness and ministry would have to start from the beginning again. But God was alive and well in this land so devastated and oppressed. Remnants of the church were still there! There was a deep spiritual hunger that only God could satisfy. Albania's communist masters may have proclaimed him dead, but God was alive and already at work!

Respect Christian Ministries
That Preexist One's Own Mission Outreach

Some of the earlier evangelical missionaries who initiated ministry in Albania failed to recognize this active presence of God at work. They were not prepared to accept his presence in the historic Christian churches. Christianity was Albania's spiritual heritage from the very beginning of the Christian era. While the Christian church had split in the early years of the second millennium of Christianity, both the Orthodox Church and the Roman Catholic Church were active in Albania during the second millennium. A few resident Protestant missionaries started Bible translation and distribution ministries in the early part of the nineteenth century, and resident missionaries had been active for several decades prior to World War II. Fifty years of atheism could not destroy all of this! In their haste to begin evangelical ministry, many groups were extremely insensitive to the presence of these historic Christian churches. Some openly opposed those who identified themselves as Orthodox or Catholic and diligently worked to convert them to their evangelical brand of Christianity.

We must be careful not to assume that only those of our theological persuasion are the only followers of God's truth in Jesus Christ. While our mission efforts must be firmly grounded in truth, we need to humbly recognize that all truth is not understood from the same theological perspective. In a country where Orthodox and Roman Catholic Christians have paid a great price for their faith, we need to be open to learn from them at the same time we share with them what is best in our evangelical understanding of our faith. Sometimes as missionaries and mission leaders we need a rebirth of the kind of humility demonstrated by the prophet Jeremiah:

This is what the LORD says:

> "Let not the wise man boast of his wisdom
>   or the strong man boast of his strength
>   or the rich man boast of his riches,
> but let him who boasts boast about this:
>   that he understands and knows me,
> That I am the LORD, who exercises kindness,

> justice and righteousness on earth,
> for in these I delight,"

declares the LORD. (Jeremiah 9:23–24)

Start Ministry with What
You Know How to Do Best

When a congregation plans to develop leadership for field mission outreach, it should ask several critical questions to help clarify its ministry identity: What are our strengths and our weaknesses? What experiences have we already had that will help inform our planned actions in this new mission outreach? What resources do we have available to help us persevere in our chosen task? What are the professional skills we will need from others? What human resource pool can we draw upon within our congregation to provide both the leadership and the in-country staff members needed to accomplish the task we are undertaking? How will we evaluate ministry progress and to whom, other than ourselves, will we become accountable?

While John and Lynn conducted various evangelistic outreaches and initiated the first steps in new church development, we undertook a congregational resource inventory. We identified our strength that could be most helpful in this new ministry. As a church located just off the campus of the University of Washington, we have developed strong student ministries and program skills. Each Tuesday evening more than one thousand students gather in Larson Hall to sing praises and to pray, to engage in serious Bible study and to share Communion together. One hundred fifty student leaders have been trained to lead in ministries with other university students. Each year several hundred students serve in short-term cross-cultural outreach ministries. Scores of other students commit to a more intensive World Deputation program. Ministering to university students is surely one of our strengths. We concluded that this was a good place for our Albanian ministry to begin.

Kevin, Sean, and Dan had all served in student leadership roles. They had completed their undergraduate studies and were interested in volunteering abroad for a one-year assignment in student ministry. While other European locations for their ministry were being considered, I visited Albania to see if this might be the right place for our congregation to begin direct ministry.

On the last leg of the outbound journey I was flying from Budapest to Tirana. After some time of flying in silence, I turned to the man seated next to me in the crowded plane and asked, "Do you speak English?"

"A little," he answered.

I sensed that he knew more English than he was ready to admit. "Are you Hungarian or Albanian?" I inquired. He informed me that he was Albanian, and when I asked about his profession he told me that he was a professor at the University of Tirana. In fact, he was the head of the department of philosophy and had been sent by the newly elected noncommunist government to study in the field of ethics and government morality!

"We have lived under fascism and then communism for more than fifty years," the professor observed. "These forms of government have given us absolutely no moral basis for our national existence. If we do not develop a clear pathway of moral and ethical decision making, we will only repeat the mistakes of yesterday all over again tomorrow."

Was there any doubt that God was confirming for me our mission elders' decision to invest our first efforts and energy in university student ministry? Professor Arian Starova offered his friendship and his relationships at the university to help us begin campus student ministry that first fall. By previous arrangement, five days later I met our three willing workers in Thessalonica, Greece, to inform them that Albania would be open as a place for their missionary service. In my first visit I was able to arrange visas for them and sent them off on a bus across that national border only so recently opened to begin their first year's ministry. We had started ministry in Albania with the type of ministry best known to us.

Build Upon Your Existing Relationships

InterVarsity's U.S. director, Dr. Steve Hayner, once served as university pastor to our congregation. We were familiar and comfortable with InterVarsity's style of ministry. Upon returning from Albania I called Steve to tell him of our interest in beginning student ministry in Albania. I shared the unique circumstances that had brought our congregation to Albania and told him of Dan, Sean, and Kevin, who were now our *resident* university student workers in Tirana.

"Steve, I don't believe in lone rangers in kingdom ministry," I confessed. "We are just a local congregation working with our local university campus. InterVarsity is a specialist in Christian ministry to university communities. Would InterVarsity be willing to go into partnership with us in opening campus ministry in Albania?" Steve quickly expressed both willingness and excitement at the prospect of this shared ministry. But he also admitted that InterVarsity had no experience in forming a partnership with a specific congregation.

"Draw up a concept paper or a suggested contract for this partnership," suggested Steve. He explained to me the nature of InterVarsity's relationship with the International Fellowship of Evangelical Students (IFES) in Europe. He told me whom I should contact in the London office and explained further how IFES normally began student work in countries that were new to their particular ministry.

Calls were made, discussions ensued, and preliminary agreements were drawn up among the three partners: University Presbyterian Church, InterVarsity Christian Fellowship in the U.S., and the International Fellowship of Evangelical Students in Europe. We all knew that we were exploring new ground in this unique ministry relationship. Now, after eight years of shared ministry, our partnership clearly shows the value of linking congregational ministry with specialized ministries so that each might strengthen the other. Today on the campus of the University of Tirana and at campuses in Elbasan, Durres, Gjirokaster, and Vlora a national student movement has developed. Building an effective partnership between a congregation and an experienced network of professional student ministries made it possible to accomplish so much more than either of us could have done alone. In its second year of ministry this international partnership afforded the opportunity for Albanian students, isolated for more than two generations from any contact with the outside world, to participate in student conferences with other Christian university students in Europe.

Develop Empowering Partnerships

Fortunately, the earliest missionaries to Albania in the 1990s understood the importance of working together. There were the needs of representing evangelicals before government and coordinating the relief efforts, so important in those first days of Albanian freedom. The Albanian Encouragement Project (AEP) evolved as that representative and coordinating group. As the AEP partnership developed, a whole range of services were provided to individual missionaries and to sponsoring mission agencies.

University Presbyterian Church was not a mission agency, but because we were fielding one of the larger missionary forces, AEP invited us into full membership along with other groups such as Campus Crusade, European Baptist Union, Frontiers, and other traditional mission sending agencies.

As a mission-mobilized congregation, we began ministry in Albania committed to interdependence rather than independence. We did not want to end up just doing our own thing! Other Presbyterian congregations had heard of opportunities for ministry in this Balkan country and expressed their desire to join us in this unique mission endeavor. We made initial attempts to contact our denomination's foreign mission body. At the same time, key denominational mission leaders were calling for increased cooperation between our denomination's mission structures and local congregation-based mission initiatives. This gave us an opportunity to build on each other's strengths. Our congregation's mission leadership felt a clear call to Albania. Our denominational leaders were committed to mission policies that had been carefully developed over two hundred years of mission history and service. We set out to work together in this creative new partnership.

Cultivate an Ecumenical Spirit

I was just completing my breakfast in the coffee shop of the Hotel Tirana when I looked across the room and saw a man wearing what appeared to be a clergy collar. I crossed the room and introduced myself, acknowledging that he appeared to be a "man of the cloth."

"I'm Father Martin Ritsi, an Orthodox priest from San Clemente, California. I have come to serve the Orthodox Church and the people of Albania."

I told him that I was a Presbyterian mission pastor also interested in ministry here in Albania. That began a rather prolonged conversation. He discovered that I had taught at Fuller Seminary and informed me that he was a graduate of Fuller Seminary's School of World Mission.

"Do you know Dr. Paul Pierson? He is my spiritual mentor."

I assured him that Paul was a dear friend of mine. We then sat for more than an hour sharing concerns for the spiritual needs of the people of Albania and sharing dreams of what it might look like for Presbyterians and Orthodox Christians to work together. Eventually I needed to leave for the airport, so we exchanged business cards and promised to keep in touch. That was the beginning of both a friendship and a working relationship. This relationship now includes other Orthodox Christians. I have learned so much from Archbishop Anastasias Yanaloutos, Father Martin, Father Luke, and my other Orthodox friends. As I have become better informed in Orthodox theology, spirituality, and liturgy, my personal spiritual life has been challenged and has grown.

But I was unprepared for the firestorm of opposition that broke out in certain quarters of the evangelical missionary community because of my friendship and partnership with Orthodox Christians. Ethnic, historical, political, and ecclesiological objections were raised. Sharing ministry with a Christian group aligned with the World Council of Churches (WCC) was anathema to some more separatist groups. (How they were able to overlook our Presbyterian connection to the WCC remains a mystery to me!) But how dare we as evangelicals enter a new country as missionaries while ignoring those who are a part of its Christian history. Albanian Christianity was born during apostolic times. The apostle Paul spoke of his ministry there: ". . . so that from Jerusalem and as far around as Illyricum I have fully proclaimed the good news of Christ. Thus I make it my ambition to proclaim the good news, not where Christ has already been named, so that I do not build on someone else's foundation" (Romans 15:19–20). Modern Albanians are the direct descendants of the Illyrians! The Christian presence in Albania was minuscule for years but developed during the time of Byzantine Christian expansion.

Now for more than five hundred years, Albanian Orthodox Christians have remained faithful to Jesus Christ even during times of intense pressure from the ruling Ottoman Empire to convert to Islam. Many sacrificed their lives while they remained faithful to their Christian witness. During the atheistic and oppressive regime of Enver Hoxha, Orthodox churches were destroyed or seized by the government for use as gymnasiums and warehouses. Their priests were killed and their most faithful believers imprisoned for long years. After those fifty years it appeared as though their communist masters had almost succeeded in destroying the church. If ever there was a suffering and persecuted church needing the prayers and active concern and involvement from other followers of Jesus, it was the Orthodox Church of Albania. The divisions that now separate evangelicals from Orthodox Christians are more a confession of our sinful humanity than they are a confession of faith!

Attempting to form a meaningful partnership has not been easy, not for us and certainly not for the leadership of the Orthodox churches. Well-meaning but poorly informed missionaries from Western nations focused many of their evangelistic efforts on proselytizing traditional Orthodox Christians. Ignoring the historical presence of this national church and overlooking the deep stream of Christian faith that marked its best informed believers, much evangelical mission activity marginalized that 20 percent of Albanian society that identified itself as Orthodox Christian. These attitudes and practices did not go unnoticed by the godly

Archbishop Anastasias. While he was trying to rebuild a persecuted and almost obliterated national church, these "cowboys from the West" were actively recruiting Orthodox believers to leave their church and become part of the newly emerging evangelical community rather than encouraging them to grow their faith within their traditional church. It is certainly unfair to accuse all evangelical missionaries of behaving in this manner. However, those who did were of significant enough number to contribute to building walls of distrust and misunderstanding that will take years to tear down.

With an evangelical commitment to ecumenism, we were determined to make our partnership with the Orthodox Church function. This was essential in order to maintain the integrity of our Christian witness in a Muslim country. We had something of great value to share with the Orthodox, while at the same time we had so much to learn from them. During succeeding years, Presbyterian missionaries have worked alongside Orthodox missionaries to jointly proclaim in both word and deed that Jesus Christ is Lord! We have developed mutual respect and understanding for each other's unique contribution, a contribution rooted in our different religious traditions. In this ministry partnership we have become together much more than either of us could have become alone. Because of this creative partnership, we joined forces with the United Bible Society to organize the Interconfessional Bible Society of Albania, an ecumenical ministry partnership of Orthodox, Roman Catholic, and Evangelical church leaders committed to the goal of translating, publishing, and distributing the scriptures in Albania. In overcoming our suspicions in this cooperative ecumenical partnership, we discovered that far more unites us than divides us. Albania, recovering from decades of atheistic Marxism and pressured by the growth of militant Islam, desperately needs this kind of united Christian witness.

Keep the Home Team Fully Involved

In congregation-based mission it is extremely important to keep the home team fully informed and fully engaged in the shared mission. Here are some principles we have discovered that help us keep this linkage healthy and meaningful:

1. Provide multiple opportunities for the home mission leaders and the mission volunteers to share their experiences with the congregation. A brief witness in one of our Sunday worship services has often been the most effective means to accomplish this. "Why did you go? How did your experience impact your personal life? What message would you like to share with your brothers and sisters here in the congregation?" These questions have been helpful in keeping the witness relational, focused, and challenging to those who hear it.

2. Develop means to communicate the mission project through the church newspaper, worship bulletin inserts, maps, picture displays, and other media available to you.

3. Encourage the formation of a support group to meet together regularly in order to maintain project interest and provide prayer support. This same group will often include the most faithful financial supporters of the project.

4. Implement your mission strategy in such a way that it does not become the responsibility of your sponsoring mission committee alone. Create opportunities for other groups in your church to participate fully in the project. Children love to participate in a project that will link them directly with children in the host country. A youth or college group may desire to participate in a well-planned short-term mission activity. Small Bible study or interest

groups will feel more involved by focusing on the ministry and needs of one of the field workers.

5. Create opportunities to share special field prayer requests in the regular prayer time of your worship service.

6. Offer a multiplicity of opportunities for members to become involved with the project financially. Identify specific opportunities or needs that will appeal to different constituencies.

7. Maintain an effective feedback system for those most interested in the mission outreach. Solicit them for ideas. Share with them results. Provide them with as much cultural and project information as possible.

Never Limit Yourselves
in Experiencing What God Can Do

Had our congregation never attempted to initiate field ministry like we did in Albania, we never could have become the mission-mobilized congregation we are now. I have never participated in any strategy or activity that has made mission come alive for me personally and for our congregation collectively more than this mission outreach. This scope of outreach is probably not possible for every congregation, but even the smallest congregation can link with others in order to experience a hands-on mission. Learn from history, borrow the ideas of others, practice effective missiological principles that have been field tested by others more experienced than yourself. Most importantly, rely on the wisdom that comes from God and the empowerment of his Spirit. It is well worth the risk and the effort. It has kept my personal missionary fires stoked and has increased my effectiveness as a missionary practitioner rather than as a mission philosopher. Most of all, it has blessed the members of our congregation.

8

Creating a Supportive
Mission Organization

*W*hen meeting with church mission committees I am most frequently asked, "What percentage of your church's income is set apart for mission?" I always answer: "Wrong question!" This is a poor evaluative tool for a congregation's mission interest. It is possible to give half of the church's entire income to mission and still have an ineffective mission outreach that neither mobilizes large numbers of the congregation for personal mission nor makes any particular mission activity effective. Funding for mission outreach is important, but it is not a guarantor of success. Never evaluate the strength of your congregation's commitment to mission primarily by the percentage of income provided for supporting your mission outreach. Instead, if a highly mobilized membership is a stated goal of your church, then evaluate the strength of your mission outreach by the number of lay volunteers involved in planning and implementing the congregation's mission strategy.

Measure your success by evaluating the depth of cross-cultural penetration mission volunteers are able to achieve in their city and by the mission partnerships that are formed. It is relatively easy to plan strategies for ministry. It is more difficult to open doors for lay people to discover and deploy their particular gifts and vision. We need to make certain that volunteers have been properly trained to minister appropriately and compassionately whether their outreach is sheltering street people, visiting prisoners, empowering those trapped by welfare to gain better control over their lives, or providing compassion and service to those who suffer with HIV/AIDS. Mission leadership should be certain that all mission outreaches that we are committed to support are biblical, culturally sensitive, and linked in partnership with Christian churches and ministries already present here at home or in a host country. Then we need to develop financial policies that encourage people to support those mission causes or missionaries of special concern to them. I want to surround the congregation with positive opportunities to invest time and money to mission outreach. The structures we create can stifle involvement or they can empower and facilitate the mission passion and energy already present in the congregation.

Seven Guiding Principles
for Organizational Development

There are no real absolutes in developing structures for mission support. Every congregation has its own culture, traditions, and resources. The size of the congregation will most certainly influence the nature of structures. The traditions of church governance vary from egalitarian approaches to rigidly structured hierarchical systems. In structuring your congregation's mission activities, familiarize yourself with the power structures and the decision-making processes of your church. Then build and adapt mission structures that will best embody your mission statement and purposes. Here are a few basic principles that help define our congregation's mission. I have seen them prove effective in other congregation-based mission programs in which there are significant differences in both theology and governing principles and practices.

1. Develop mission structures (committees, departments, task forces, commissions, etc.) that empower the maximum number of congregational members to share in congregational mission outreach.

2. Identify your people of vision and passion—members with a heart for mission and a passion to serve. Equip and deploy these volunteers to work in the areas of mission concern that are closest to their passion rather than in areas where the mission is shortest on volunteers! If leaders exercise total ownership over the entire visioning and planning process, then expect a passion deficit in your volunteers. A fundamental principle that informs my entire mission planning is this: *People commit themselves most to those things they are a part of creating.*

3. Create welcoming structures that encourage volunteers to be personally involved in mission planning. Organize them around visions and tasks they feel most committed to rather than recruiting others to support your plans. Hold them responsible to their commitment. Support them with the resources they need to accomplish their goals.

4. Assure that every mission organizational structure empowers participants at every level of decision making. Delegated project responsibility must include delegated authority for those volunteers to maintain strong feelings of involvement and ownership.

5. Develop supporting programs that will nurture your volunteer participants and keep them emotionally and spiritually healthy. Avoid burnout by providing friendly ways to exit from volunteer leadership at appropriate times. I encourage all volunteers, in every area of congregational life, to serve in one position no longer than three years before either moving to another area of interest or

taking a year's sabbatical from that particular service. This prevents ministry fatigue, keeps vision and passion fresh, and discourages possessive ownership over any church ministry.

6. Provide a variety of opportunities for congregational information sharing and program feedback. If a specific program or outreach has been promoted and funded, it is important for those who participated either as volunteers or as contributors to receive regular status reports. Such project reporting is needed to assure continued congregational participation and support.

7. Be generous in affirming the efforts of each participant at every level of involvement and service. Maintain a positive approach to problem solving. Bruce Larson frequently reminded us that "it takes ten *atta boys* to cancel out one *you jerk!*" Too often in congregational ministry the words of encouragement and affirmation are much slower in coming than words of complaint and criticism.

Understanding the Congregation's Role

No congregation, regardless of its size, should consider itself an adequate replacement for more traditional mission agencies and denominational mission structures. Engaging in mission and serving cross-culturally necessitate a broader range of experience than is available in any single congregation. Church size, however, makes some difference in how that congregation will organize the mission task. The larger the congregation and the more committed its leadership to cross-cultural ministry, the more complex its mission organizational structures will become. Whereas a very large congregation with significant human and financial resources may plan and supervise a major mission outreach program locally or globally, it will still lack the historical perspective and the missiological experience of traditional mission structures. Zeal and creativity are not substitutes for the experience gained from long years of service. (Coalitions of smaller congregations tightly knit together by shared mission vision and purpose can accomplish together what none of them could accomplish alone. In our presbytery, groups of congregations have banded together to accomplish a singular mission goal.) Whether the congregation is large or small, there are certain commonalities in the mission task, such as

- uniting the congregation in its shared mission challenge;
- providing the congregation with accurate and challenging mission information;
- making available greater financial resources than those currently budgeted;
- recruiting missionaries and candidates, and training and equipping them spiritually and financially;
- forming partnerships in the mission-targeted locations;
- conducting needs and resource assessments before the initiation of outreach projects;
- measuring ideas for new mission personnel and program opportunities against existing mission objectives;
- making sure that mission volunteers are well trained, adequately equipped for service, and pastorally supported while serving.

Before launching a particular mission outreach project, clearly identify traditional mission agencies, parachurch organizations, and denominational mission structures that can help support your outreach efforts. These agencies need to share with you in the planning in order for them to feel empowered as full partners. While our church has enough human and financial resources to undertake major mission programs, we still remain linked with traditional mission-sending agencies and denominational mission structures. These help us maintain accountability to the larger church and assure quality of ministry consistent with the best current missiological practice. We are not a substitute for the historic mission agencies or denominational mission efforts; we supplement the mission efforts of others while successfully developing our congregation's interest and ownership in mission outreach through direct involvement in planning and implementation. Our model is not for every congregation, nor should it be. But it has served us well and is offered as one working model. In presenting a model I am not talking about committees or departments. Structures and policies we have developed from our experience have helped us to minimize committee work and maximize ministry outreach. While certain departmentalization or committee structures can be helpful, if they hinder ministry and become institutionalized, these structures will become more an obstacle than an aid to mission.

Energizing the Laity for Outreach Planning

While our mission outreach ministries have increased fourfold over the past ten years, today we rely much less on traditional mission structures and much more on individual task forces of lay leaders organized around very specific outreach objectives. Where once a committee of six to eight persons made the program decisions for all our global outreach programs, currently there are more than one hundred highly motivated lay members giving leadership to a score of task forces. Each of these task forces has risen from the dreams and creative energies of their lay leaders. While there is an excellent accountability process in place for these task forces, we have no predetermined structural or policy criteria they must duplicate. Our global task forces focus on specific ministry areas where we have a strong commitment to mission funding and missionary personnel: Albania, Russia, Romania, Bosnia/ Croatia, India, Kyrgyzstan, Eastern Mediterranean, Latin America, the Middle East, and Haiti. While each of these was created by different circumstances, there is commonality among them all:

- a lay person initiated the task force;
- the task force is led by laity, not by staff;
- the task force is solely responsible for developing its own funding;
- the focus of the task force is consistent with ministry values and priorities that the mission leadership has already committed to;
- often our missionary volunteers were already serving in a particular field before the task force was begun;
- in each country or area where our denominational mission is active, the congregation's mission activity is intentionally linked to the denominational activity;
- in several countries where our denominational mission was not active we were able to provide leadership for it to become active;
- the task forces are not created as permanent committees, but remain in place only as long as the original mission purpose or focus is served;
- each task force maintains accountability with the congregation through mission department administrative structures already in place.

In just a few years, these task forces have revolutionized how the mission department conducts its affairs. For years the department met once a month, and most of our energies were focused on planning and approving the budget. Twenty to thirty lay members controlled the mission process for the entire congregation. The task forces have changed all of that! The global task forces alone involve more than 120 lay members. They all feel a high sense of ownership over a particular ministry and possess a good working knowledge of the particular field their task force serves. As effective interpreters and motivators of their program they reach a much broader audience within the congregation than a single traditional mission conference would reach. And these energized lay people are great fundraisers! Just one-half of these task forces this year will raise more funds for their mission projects than the entire general ministry fund provides for all of our mission activity. Since they began, these lay-led task forces have more than doubled the finances available for mission outreach! Remember, mission belongs to the *whole* church, not just to the mission committee or department. Mission volunteers exist to help the whole church achieve its mission outreach goals. Multiplying lay involvement will always multiply the resources available to expand mission outreach.

A Great Divide or a Helpful Division?

Many congregations include persons who desire to apply mission outreach only to their home community: "There is so much that needs to be done right here at home, so many people needing help, so many needs to be met; we should meet these needs first before going somewhere else in the world!" Others will argue just as forcefully for prioritizing foreign or global mission: "There are so many who have never heard yet of Jesus' love for them in a manner that is culturally relevant. We have so many opportunities and resources and they have so few; we should give first preference to the unreached people." The heat generated by these arguments tends to create more steam than light! But mission must never become an either/or proposition. To take mission to the ends of the earth but neglect human need and spiritual darkness within our own community is just as irresponsible as focusing all of our efforts and resources locally, believing that we must first take care of our own before reaching out to others.

We have found it helpful to divide the task between urban mission and global mission. The division has to do with location rather than with nature of ministry. The task of mission always remains the same: *To plan and supervise the development and deployment of human, financial, and partnership resources for cross-cultural ministry opportunities locally, nationally, and globally.* Both tasks are profoundly cross-cultural. Both are intentional and specialized. Both focus on ministries outside the walls of the church and usually outside the family structures of our congregation. In our church it is the Department of Urban and Global Mission that is charged specifically with sharing our Christian life and witness beyond those we normally serve in our regular church programs. This is cross-cultural mission, as distinguished from the fellowship of our monocultural worship community.

Currently there are eighteen part-time and full-time staff serving this department in addition to the more than seventy term and career mission personnel serving in twenty-seven fields and the several hundred short-term mission volunteers we send each year to serve in programs developed by our youth, university, and adult ministry departments. The reason for such a large compensated mission staff is not what you might think! We have a large staff, not to do the work of missions, but to assist and support the hundreds of mission volunteers engaged in planning and service every week. Our pastoral role in supporting our lay volunteers is at the very top of the list of our professional responsibilities.

Mission in Our Own Backyard

I remember asserting once in one of my sermons, "The integrity of our mission program will be tested and judged, not so much by what we do in the slums of Calcutta and Nairobi, but in the streets and alleyways of Seattle!" I still believe this deeply. Too often we have focused our "mission concern" on what our ethnic mix is at a typical Sunday worship service. Certainly becoming a welcoming congregation to all who enter our church doors is extremely important. But political correctness must not become the driving motivational force behind our mission strategies. The issue is not what our ethnic or racial mix is in our Sunday worship services, but rather, where are the people of God all the rest of the hours of the week? In order to transform this from a slogan to a reality, we have placed great emphasis upon creating an urban ministry focus that is effective both in identifying urgent needs in our community and then mobilizing and equipping lay people to serve effectively in these areas. Just as we have developed task forces around specific countries or regions throughout the world, we have done the same with our urban mission responsibilities. It has been exciting to see individual members of our congregation latch onto an area of need, and then for mission staff to help them develop a committed group of lay volunteers who are ready to make this particular ministry happen! Each of our urban ministry concentrations has evolved this way.

- Street Youth Ministries responded to the unique physical and spiritual needs of youth ages thirteen to seventeen who need friendship, shelter, guidance, and various forms of assistance while they try to survive life on the streets. Often these kids are "throwaway" rather than runaway kids.

- Mental Health Ministries was created to meet the needs of those suffering from mental and emotional stresses and disorders and to minister to families needing support in coping with a loved one's mental illness.
- Intentional Communities grew out of one staff member's desire to form households within our inner city where young men and women could develop a community of faith and discover their ministries right where they live.
- Language Institute for Refugees was started to meet the specific language needs of a large group of Cambodian refugees. The program has developed to the point where it can meet those same needs in other refugee communities. It also helps other congregations develop English language programs in their neighborhoods.
- Project Farewell was initiated by a key group of lay volunteers who felt that the church has a special role to play in assisting individuals and families in their transition from welfare to empowered living.

Create Your Own

Don't borrow our organizational model for your congregation's mission outreach needs. It won't work! Rather, evaluate your own mission objectives and identify the human and financial resources needed and available for the task. Then organize your own lay resources in order to provide opportunities for highly focused volunteer involvement in decision making and a high level of ownership over the outreach programs that develop out of these networks of individuals who share a common purpose and passion. Our staffing pattern serves us well but keeps on changing as the mission changes and expands. It merely illustrates what our congregation has done in order to clarify and focus our mission energies, mobilize our laity for mission outreach ministries, and create greater opportunities for financial investment in mission. Each congregation with professional mission staff will need to develop both the departmental organization and specific position descriptions to meet its unique needs and to utilize its laity's skills and experience. If the mobilization of laity for ministry is a top priority for your church, then providing these lay volunteers with the professional staff that will help them achieve their ministry goals is one of the best investments any congregation can make. Rather than hiring staff departmentally, churches should hire staff functionally; there are preachers, teachers, musicians, *and* there are resource mobilizers! Mobilizing its lay members for ministry and then helping them to develop the human and financial resources necessary to implement the ministry plan should be a top priority for any healthy and growing congregation. And *healthy* congregations are *growing* congregations!

9

Mobilizing the
Financial Resources

I was in a big hurry! I had led worship in three of
our five regular worship services and had just two
hours left to drive home, grab a bite to eat, head to
the airport, and catch a Frankfurt-bound flight. After
an overnight in Frankfurt, I would be off to Russia,
Turkey, and Albania. And I hadn't even started to
pack my suitcase yet! As I was trying to escape
unnoticed out the back door of the chancel our executive pastor interrupted my departure: "There's a
couple just outside the door who wish to speak to
you for just a minute. They said that they were really
moved by the lay witness's interview in the worship
service. They feel that God is directing them to give
a generous contribution to help assist the church's
Albanian mission outreach that the witness spoke of
this morning."

Rather impatiently I reversed course and returned
to meet the couple with the contribution. (When not
in a hurry I am usually quite interruptible when
tempted by some possible mission funding!) They
were standing in the doorway waiting. "Walk along
with me to my study so we can talk on the way," I
suggested. I could sense that they had been deeply
touched by Art and Eloise Ware's interview. This
missionary couple had just been evacuated from

Albania by a U.S. Marine helicopter a few days before. The country was in total chaos. Marauding bands of hooligans had looted weapons of every caliber and description from the country's military armories. The Wares had barely escaped with their lives.

Before we reached my study the waiting couple gave me their contribution and said, "God has blessed us in our business. We regularly give to the church, but we've never really made a special gift that really stretches us. God told us this morning that this was the time to do it! We would like at least a major portion of the gift to go toward meeting some of the emergency needs in Albania." I thanked them for their gift and hurried back to my office. They followed. (I hadn't noticed the amount of the two checks. That's not really the proper thing to do!) We stood and chatted for a few minutes and I apologized for being in a hurry.

"If you don't mind," explained the husband, "Mary would like to have $5000 of her gift go to the organ fund, and I would like $6000 to go toward our commitment to the building fund." Now they really had my attention! At this point I thought I had better take a look at the two checks. While I was glad the organ and building funds had just received a large gift, I was concerned that there might not be enough of the remaining contribution for Albania. I looked at the checks and, to my surprise, each was for $20,000. I couldn't suppress my exclamation of joy— $29,000 of their contribution was designated for me to take to Albania!

Their gift reminded me of the enormous changes this congregation had made to facilitate such giving. Just a few years ago members were discouraged from designating any of their contributions, which were all to be given to the general operating fund. Designated gifts were sometimes even returned to the contributor with encouragement for them to contribute to this fund, or to send the designated gift directly to the ministry they wished to support. The prevailing belief governing our contribution policy was that if the church ever opened the door to designated giving, the general fund of the church would suffer proportionately. I have heard this myth repeated by scores of church leaders who have consulted with me concerning church finances. Unfortunately, financial leaders are too often guided only by years of tradition of one designation for all contributions and one method for receiving those funds—the offering plate on Sunday morning.

Decently and in Order

If you are a Presbyterian you undoubtedly know that everything in Presbyterian culture and tradition is to be done "decently and in order." Every congregation has developed its own systems and policies to regulate the orderliness of the financial affairs of the congregation. Our congregation's faithful giving made it possible for the budget to climb upward each year. Our people are a generous people! But always the budgeting process and the annual stewardship campaign seemed to leave leaders emotionally drained and spiritually depleted. We all knew that when the process was completed it would be followed by weekly measurement of congregational performance, hoping that budget expectations were being met. The church's budget became the focal point for understanding God's faithfulness and our obedience in contributing generously of the resources needed for the church's ministries. But budgets are boring! Is it any wonder that we grow either weary or bored with annual stewardship campaigns! We take impressive measures to stimulate regular and faithful giving. But little enthusiasm is generated when the congregation perceives that they are merely underwriting budgets and paying bills.

Like many congregations, our church had learned to depend upon a rather traditional stewardship campaign in order to assure the congregation that there would be enough funds available for next year's ministry. Some years ago our senior pastor asked me to work with the congregation's stewardship committee to reexamine our approach to this annual event. (Isn't it interesting that we often refer to this event as a *campaign,* a military term that has more the connotation of coercion and capitulation than creative planning and enthusiastic enlistment?) But our congregation was no different from others. We, too, believed the myth that it is impossible to have a financial operating plan for the congregation without an effective pledge system to solicit the congregation's contributions for the next fiscal year's operations. Yet I know of no manufacturing business or marketing enterprise that could succeed if the only way they could develop a financial operating plan was to get their customers to pledge in advance how much of their product or service they would promise to purchase!

Every congregation doing financial planning has the same resources available to it as does any business. Those market indicators of community growth, inflation, and employment that are used in business are available to the congregation for their financial planning. Faith is activated when we move beyond these financial indicators and projections to try and discern God's will for our giving in next year's financial planning. How much beyond last year's financial performance are we ready to trust God for in the coming year? This reasonable and sensible approach to financial planning and budget making does *not* require pledging. In my years of pastoral work I have observed that many church members do not like pledging. They feel that giving is a very personal matter, or want to follow the biblical injunction not to "let your right hand know what your left hand is doing." However, most of these members are quite willing to make a time-limited pledge to a special project or fund, while resisting pledging as a means to secure funds for the regular ministry operations of the congregation.

It was not easy to move our congregation or its leadership to this new way of thinking. So we began to make some very important changes slowly and incrementally. (Remember, Presbyterians do things decently and in order!) Beginning in the first year of change, we retained our traditional pledge card, which requested the same information: "How much do you plan to give next year to the church's ministry and mission?" But instead of having members prepare this card to turn in on "Pledge Sunday," we added a tear-off supplement to the card. By signing this supplement, the contributors acknowledged that they as individuals or families had prayerfully considered their giving responsibilities for the coming year, and that they desired to be counted on as a "giver of record." They kept the part of the card that contained the specific amount of their pledge as a daily reminder of their commitment. Through the public presentation of the tear-off part of the card, we retained the tradition in which contributors actually physically come forward with the dedication of their offerings as an act of commitment. In this way we kept traditionalists comfortable but also taught the congregation that pledge amounts were not necessary for the financial well-being of the church. This new method prepared us for the next step of change. And the church did not collapse financially without this information!

The next year our pledge card was redesigned. Rather than asking the traditional question regarding next year's planned contribution, the card asked a much more significant question—a question that was consistent with our understanding of biblical stewardship: "Believing the words of James 1:17, 'Every generous act of giving, with every perfect gift, is from above,' what percentage of next year's income do I (we) believe is God's will for us to retain for our personal and family use?" There was room for a signature after the amount was written in. But this card was never intended to be turned in to the financial office; rather, it remained with the contributor as a powerful reminder of God's demands for accountability as stewards of his treasure. We are not merely custodians of God's tithe and our offerings; we are stewards of all God has entrusted to us, accountable to God alone for how we steward his treasure.

Conducting our annual stewardship planning in this new way had a profound impact on our members as they thought through the issues of faithful and obedient stewardship. The stewardship committee has supported this approach with various stewardship information aids that help each member consider not only all the options of where one can give, but *how* one can give. Rather than limiting our thinking to pledge cards and offering plates, we can think seriously about all of our financial resources and how these can be more effectively offered to the work of the kingdom of God.

Since we made these changes in how the congregation does financial planning, there has been a dramatic increase in per capita giving in our regular offerings, special offerings, year-end stock gifts, wills, and bequests. Moreover, there is a level of excitement in giving that was not present before. All of our financial planning and reporting is now focused on what the congregation is accomplishing in ministry rather than upon the needs we have to underwrite budgets and meet expenses. I present this information, not just as a mere technique in how to change financial planning, but to underscore the importance for Christians to begin thinking differently about money. Until we begin to think differently, our mission opportunities will always be underfunded. And much worse, our vision will be limited. We will not see what God sees. We will not understand that most of our financial problems are within the capacity of our congregation to be filled.

Mission Brings New Financial Challenges

Whenever a congregation commits to expanding ministries, new financial resources are needed. Except for the most affluent congregations, the regular operational costs of the church consume most of the financial resources available through the regular tithes and offerings of the congregation. Salaries and staff benefits must be paid, buildings must be maintained, and the escalating costs of utilities, supplies, and insurance demand an ever increasing portion of available funds. With this growth in operational costs, mission budgets often constrict. Program decisions made in previous years need to be continued. Each year, less becomes available for initiating new mission outreach ministries.

After more than eighty years of ministry our congregation faced just such a crisis. Congregational members' interest in ministry had greatly expanded. Every church department was experiencing significant growth. Our commitment to minister effectively to the faculty and students of a major university stimulated new outreach ideas and expanded spheres of ministry for this large student population. While we were deeply committed to these ministries, the financial resources to fund new challenges were not available. There was nothing unique about our problem, but the leadership wanted to do more than simply acknowledge it. We were ready to search for creative solutions—solutions that would stretch our faith, test our obedience, and challenge those artificial limitations we had unknowingly created.

Just as we discovered that our means to develop funding through the traditional annual stewardship campaign had placed limitations on the congregation's generosity, I am convinced that we are guilty of placing another limitation on giving. This limitation has to do with how we interpret "tithing" in the contemporary American church. In much preaching, tithing—contributing 10 percent of one's income—is held up as the ultimate biblical principle for stewardship. We need to develop a much deeper understanding: "From everyone to whom much has been given, much will be required; and from the one to whom much has been entrusted, even more will be demanded" (Luke 12:48). All Christians need to learn how to translate this principle within the context of our economic affluence. For many North American Christians, tithing becomes the ultimate cop-out! Rather than moving toward a principle of proportionate giving (giving according to the amount we have received), we promote a level of giving that is often far below the capacity of many of us to give. After all, most of us tip our waiters more than 10 percent! Then when we consider that the average American church member contributes significantly less than 10 percent, our underperformance should be a major concern.

Perhaps because of this low performance, pleading with people to give 10 percent becomes the focus for our wishful thinking. Surely this is one of the reasons that our affluence, rather than blessing and resourcing the ministries of the kingdom of God, binds us by a materialism that demands little sacrifice and that saps our spiritual energy and limits the church's mission. There is something patently unfair about holding up a standard of stewardship that demands from the widow, the orphan, and the stranger the same level of giving that we place upon those of us who are gainfully employed, and who often are compensated at levels that exceed the legitimate needs of person and family. It was the Old Testament tithe that, rather than being the ultimate standard of sacrifice, was used to support those very widows, orphans, and strangers. Proportional giving has always been God's standard for faithful stewardship. When our churches are challenged to live according to this standard we will find that we have abundant resources for local ministry and global outreach. In addition, our individual lives will be blessed and enriched spiritually as we experience God's faithfulness in providing all of our needs (personal and congregational) "according to the riches of his glory in Christ Jesus." When we present the mission challenge in need of financial resources, we need to remind our congregation of God's unchanging promise: "Give, and it will be given to you. A good measure, pressed down, shaken together, running over, will be put into your lap; for the measure you give will be the measure you get back" (Luke 6:38).

The Seven Last Words
of the Church

"We never did it that way before!" It seemed to me as though the majority of our session spoke with one voice. I had been requested to write a paper entitled, "A Creative Approach to Resource Development." I thought it was a rather brilliant paper and was not prepared to receive some of the negative responses. "Impossible!" "Improbable!" "Impractical!" "Not provable and surely unworkable!" "We never did it that way before!" The session expressed its specific objections and legitimate concerns. These were not just quick reactions to new ideas. Some perceived these new ideas as a threat to the future financial health of the congregation. Except for the most creative visionaries and wild entrepreneurs, we resist change because change is difficult. There is always something to give up in order to receive something that is new. My paper requested the session to test some old myths and then suggested some new ideas for the congregation to consider. This paper

- encouraged designated giving to outreach ministries approved by the session;
- suggested several new annual special offerings that would help underwrite specific outreach ministries;
- proposed that the congregation reconsider its historic objections to fund-raising activities;
- suggested that certain ministry interns and specialized ministry staff members whose responsibilities were either in local mission outreach or university student ministries could be funded through designated giving rather than from the limited resources of the general fund (isn't it interesting that what becomes most threatening to a congregation is the very method of fund-raising that we expect of our missionaries?);
- outlined a procedure to establish designated giving accounts for members who volunteered for professional mission service and who were responsible for raising their personal support funds.

Many churches have never challenged the cultural myth that the *spiritual* way to collect the tithes and offerings of the people is either through the weekly collection plates or by the use of the appropriate stewardship packet of offering envelopes. Test this out. You may be surprised how many members of your congregation hold this belief!

Fortunately, in my case, many members of the session were now prepared to thoughtfully consider new ideas and challenges. This paper had surfaced new ideas and challenged important issues. Some of these contemplated changes were of special significance in light of the generational changes occurring within American culture. For example, the giving motivation for baby boomers is quite different from those of their parents. Financial appeals that are made primarily by pleas for institutional loyalty are of little interest to the baby boomers, and also the baby busters and generation Xers. These members of the younger generations want to see their contributions closely related to their specific ministry interests. Institutional and denominational loyalties are almost nonexistent for these young contributors.

Once the local church or its denominational structures stood almost alone as the organizational means available to implement ministry. But since the conclusion of World War II there has been a proliferation of parachurch ministries, creative new mission agencies, and specialized ministries designed to appeal to the younger generation's ministry interests. Direct mail advertising and sophisticated fund-raising appeals compete daily for space in church members' mailboxes. These funding appeals are professionally designed and often target the ministry interests of the contributor. There is a more direct relationship between the contribution and the activity or individual the contributor wishes to support. Religious television provides potential contributors both sight and sound. Mission and ministry outreach that had seemed impossible in previous generations is now very achievable for these new mobile generations. This has increased the need to establish a direct line of communication between ministry and contributor. While a rather new concept to some, this idea of personalized contributions that encourage a direct relationship between a person's own creative ideas and concerns and the ministries she chooses to support makes very good sense. We feel a higher sense of ownership over those things we take part in creating.

I value my wife's positive comments concerning my latest sermon, but when she begins to edit my remarks, watch out! In a similar way, sometimes by the way congregations attempt to control ministry they often stifle members' interest, creativity, and ownership. Our church programs invite observers rather than involve active participants. Merely placing a lone dollar bill or a tightly sealed offering envelope into the brass offering plate does little to capture long-term ministry interest. Giving to the work of God's kingdom must be much more than a passive activity! It must possess an active component to make our appeals for contributions effective.

10

Fund-Raising or Fund-Releasing?

*F*und-raising activities were a prohibited strategy in our congregation's tradition. A few years ago our high-schoolers were prevented from holding a car wash to develop resources for one of their planned mission outreach activities. "It just isn't spiritual! The next thing you know we'll eliminate offerings and operate the church on proceeds from bingo games and raffles!" Others were less passionate in their response, but just as concerned.

I find that committed people are usually objective and innovative when we appeal to their reason, intelligence, and creativity. With this in mind, I attempted to persuade our congregation's leadership to be more open to fund-raising activities by presenting a parable to illustrate our need to reconsider our objections. In my parable, "Defending Dedicated Daisy," the title character was presented as an active but retired member of our congregation. She had been left widowed years before. Since that time she had had to exist on nothing more than her monthly minimum Social Security check. After contributing her monthly gift of 10 percent of her income, there was often not enough remaining for her to purchase some of her prescribed medications. Generic medications were still too expensive to fill the gap between her limited funds and her basic medical needs. Daisy sincerely struggled with the issue of tithing. She wanted to remain faithful to God while at the same time being realistic about her needs. The parable of Daisy's dilemma was an effective means to challenge our session members' traditional thinking. I reminded them that the Old Testament pattern of tithing provided funds primarily for the support of widows and orphans. It was not the tithes but the *special* giving of the people that built tabernacles and temples!

This parabolic Daisy experiences conflicted needs. She needs to purchase her medications, but she needs to contribute to her church according to her ability. Preaching on a universal principle of tithing for all God's children had left her with feelings of guilt. I encouraged all of us to think more clearly and creatively about this presumed conflict: "Why not encourage the church's deacons to help Daisy resolve her conflict in a more creative way? Give Daisy a little bit of shortening, a bag of flour, some sugar, and a package of chocolate chips and Daisy can bake a wicked batch of Toll House cookies. Allow our youth to sell these cookies along with the coffee we already provide to faithful worshipers. A small contribution to fund the ingredients for Daisy's cookies costs so little and would sure make the coffee hour more enjoyable. Our youth can use these funds for their mission project in Tijuana, Mexico. This will encourage them in their mission concerns and create a practical means for them to implement their missionary calling. And watch how it empowers Daisy! This will surely help her feel that she is a full contributing member of our church family!"

Somehow our materialistic way of thinking has limited our idea of church contributions to those made only in dollars and cents. The "Daisy" of the parable helped our leaders broaden their understanding of giving. Daisy's resources combined with her baking skills and available time empowered her to be just as significant a contributor as those who were able to contribute a tither's check!

No Limits to Creativity

Years have passed since this initial challenge, and our congregational giving has been radically and positively changed. No, we have not resorted to bingo games to fund our general operating needs. There are some strategies that are off-limits even to the most creative among us! But fund-raising activities have multiplied through the years. University students contribute their time and energies each year to members of the congregation who need lawns mowed, backyard weeds rooted out, prized goods stored in attics, and basements cleared of accumulated possessions that are neither needed nor valued. The going rate for this labor is ten dollars per hour. These volunteers raise more than thirty-five thousand dollars each year to fund summer World Deputation activities in many countries. Those members who host the university volunteers delight in making a new relationship with a university student, find great joy by becoming part of the students' summer outreach mission, and experience relief in seeing the most unpleasant unfinished tasks around their homes accomplished at last!

Dave is responsible for the church's mental health outreach ministry. He enlisted the entire congregation in donating their available yard sale accumulations and recruited scores of volunteers to prepare, price, and display these items, and then serve as the sales force for the First Annual UPC Parking Lot Yard Sale for Mental Health Ministries. More than seven thousand dollars was received from sales of accumulated junk. Alice funds her outreach ministry to youth involved in the drug culture by operating a used clothing store.

Our single adult ministries sponsor UPC's annual Fun Run, a ten-kilometer run participated in by hundreds of church members. Lots of calories are burned off, and more than twenty-five thousand dollars is raised each year to support adult short-term mission.

On an even larger scale, each winter our youth department sponsors a silent auction. Our senior pastor refers to the event as "UPC's premier social event of the year!" On the chosen Sunday, our largest hall is filled with an incredible variety of donated goods and services available for purchase during the silent auction. (Can you imagine proper Presbyterians sponsoring an auction that was *not* silent? Everything is done decently and in order!) The excitement is shared by the youth who labor to make the silent auction succeed and who will benefit by participating in the mission outreach funded from the auction's proceeds. This excitement is shared by the buyers who carry home a prized possession or enjoy a service that they would not usually purchase. Our members just can't resist an unbelievable bargain. I purchased a beautiful ten-speed bicycle for a final written bid of only sixty-seven dollars.

Contributors also share by offering things of value for sale, thereby discovering one more way to invest in ministry. Quite a number of church members own recreational property and weekend getaways. A week's vacation or a weekend retreat in one of these offered properties has become one of the hottest ticket items at each year's auction. One of our most successful sale items each year is contributed by a talented young woman who offers a gourmet dinner for eight persons, accompanied by selections from C. S. Lewis read by our senior pastor. This year it sold for more than six thousand dollars! Despite limited artistic skills, I even hand-painted a coffee mug. I had been the preacher earlier that day, so I used this opportunity to invite the worshipers to the silent auction. I told them that each of their pastors had created a beautiful, personally designed coffee mug and hinted that my self-esteem was very involved in the sale of *my* coffee mug! It sold for the highest price!

Giving can be made fun for all, at the same time that the result of our giving is serious business. The more than one hundred thousand dollars raised in this year's silent auction provided funds for several hundred youth and their adult sponsors to go on an annual house-building mission trip to the slums of Tijuana. What a great mission opportunity for our youth! And what a powerful witness of Christ's love and concern for those who receive a new home while enjoying the friendships formed with students and adults who participate in this important ministry.

These are just a few examples of what has worked for us. Your church can be just as creative. Discover your best assets and resources, then make them available to be multiplied for the kingdom of God. The congregation with two hundred members has the same amount of resources and volunteers proportionately as does the congregation with four thousand members. Remember the basic principle: *People commit themselves most to those things they are a part of creating.* This is the defining principle behind every decision and activity that involves resource development. I refer to these as *fund-releasing* activities rather than *fund-raising* activities. If we truly believe what we sing, that our God "owns the cattle on a thousand hills, the wealth in every mine," and if our theology of stewardship is shaped by the truth that "every perfect gift is from above, coming from the Father of lights," then we should surrender our traditional inhibitions concerning stewardship methodology and open wide ourselves to God's creativity. We will become far more creative and resourceful when we offer our laity meaningful ways to become more involved financially.

In the past I often felt inhibited in challenging people

to use all of their resources wisely and creatively. Prevailing American cultural attitudes toward money mislead us into believing that these resources are ours. ("My finances are a very private matter!") However, when our lives are guided by the truth of God's ownership over *all* that we possess, not just over the tithe, then our inhibitions in mentioning money will be overcome. We are not violating any person's privacy. We are only discussing together what already belongs to God. We are offering guidance and support to those who wish to handle their personal stewardship of resources more generously and responsibly. This fresh insight into stewardship will serve to revolutionize our worship. We will more clearly identify what it is or whom it is that we worship.

This has been freeing and fulfilling for our congregation. Those who argued against designing creative giving opportunities were wrong. Our best financial analysts and consultants have crunched the numbers each year since the church committed to this new pathway of stewardship and can easily demonstrate how these activities and designated gifts have provided upward momentum to the regular giving of our tithes and offerings. In the last ten years our congregation's giving quadrupled while our membership increased by 33 percent. Neither inflation nor a booming economy is alone responsible for this increase. The increase genuinely reflects the increased involvement and commitment of our church family. They are contributing with a genuine sense of excitement about their personal connections with expanded ministry and mission outreach.

We Can Do It in New Ways

I met Aaron on my way to the finance office. He was carrying a stack of envelopes with a whole range of designated contributions in them. There were gifts for Barb in Mozambique, Ray and Sandra in Haiti, Marta in Kenya, and designated contributions for several of our partnership ministries here in Seattle. Ray and Sandra needed an updated list of their current contributors so that they might acknowledge their generosity and maintain accountability.

"Art, this new way of designated giving just isn't working!" exclaimed Aaron. "I know that the session passed an action to make this possible, but they just don't understand the problems of this increased workload for the finance office! We just don't have the staff or the volunteer hours to keep up with the work. Sorry, but things are going to have to change."

True! But what needed to change? Thinking needed to change. Outdated procedures needed to change. How we allocate resources for finance office staffing needed to change in order to keep up with the increased volume of work caused by this dramatic increase in giving. But that's not a bad problem to have! Unfortunately, our church administrator was not quite so enthusiastic. Bookkeepers are conditioned to avoid change; financial leaders create new solutions for new problems. My response to Aaron was immediate and emphatic. While acknowledging his viewpoint on the problem and endeavoring to affirm his leadership, I reminded him of the session's new commitment to encourage designated mission giving along with other creative resource development ideas. The finance department's responsibility was to make it possible for the other departments of the church to achieve their ministry goals. "What will it take for your office to provide the new services needed?" I asked. His response was immediate! He strongly implied that here was a problem without a solution: "There just aren't enough staff hours to care for this volume of giving when these gifts need to be accounted for in such a multiplicity of accounts." Keeping all the funds in one purse may be more efficient, but it kills both creativity and the interest of contributors to maintain a direct link with their supported ministry.

And why not institute a little creativity to help solve a big problem! In order to help solve this accounting problem, I suggested that the session assess a service charge of 6 percent to all designated gifts and use these funds to employ additional financial staff. A few of the elders were shocked that I, of all people, would suggest such a penalty charge! But there are added costs to support this type of giving program. When any of us support financially a missionary or parachurch ministry, our contribution is usually assessed a small service charge in order to provide the administrative and financial support needed for that ministry. In order to accommodate this broader financial participation by our congregation, why can't we do the same? I urged them to make an investment that would promote and facilitate increased interest in financially supporting mission outreach where the contributor can maintain a direct link to the supported ministry. The session approved the policy, and the finance office increased staffing hours to accommodate the increased workload. None of our missionaries or mission partnership organizations suffered any negative consequences from our decision.

This is just one of many possibilities leaders will need to consider in order to encourage new and more productive ways for doing ministry. This new policy was instituted ten years ago. More recently, the service charge has been eliminated. The spontaneous generosity of our members in contributing to *all* ministries of the congregation no longer makes this surcharge necessary. During this same period, while church membership has increased by 33 percent, giving has more than quadrupled and mission contributions have increased sixfold! The pain we experienced in changing policies and creating new procedures hardly compares with the joyful enthusiasm we all share in our increased ministries. Now only about one-third of our mission expenditures come from the traditional budgeted sources of revenue available to us a decade ago. Two-thirds of our mission outreach is now funded through designated giving and our various fund-raising activities.

Creating New Opportunities

There is no one correct way for a congregation to develop its financial policies and procedures. There is no singularly correct way to organize or supervise a congregation in meeting its mission goals and objectives. Although the Word of God never changes, our policies and procedures must change if we are going to keep in step with the times and manage congregational growth. Here are a few practical ideas we have developed to stimulate growth in interest and financial involvement for our mission outreach. These are neither sacred nor complete. They are a work in progress. Consider some examples learned from our experience, then either adapt them or create new ones so that they will work for you.

Personnel Outreach Accounts (POA)

Personnel Outreach Accounts are approved by our governing body in order to establish a way for individual friends and family members to support a commissioned UPC missionary. Upon appointment, the mission team helps the missionary establish the required level of personal support and funds needed for the mission assignment. If the candidate will serve under the supervision of a traditional mission sending agency or our denomination's mission division, the support level will be set by the sponsoring agency. If the candidate is sent directly by our congregation, then the appropriate committee will approve the requested support level. This method has succeeded beyond our expectations and has served members of our congregation very well. They enjoy this direct linkage with their missionary friend.

Ministry Outreach Accounts (MOA)

Ministry Outreach Accounts (MOA) serve much the same purpose as the POA, only they are project specific rather than personnel specific. The procedure to establish the account may be generated by either the urban or global mission sectors. Our urban mission's mandate is to support cross-cultural mission outreach here in Seattle and to work cooperatively with our local presbytery in its urban outreach. In global mission we partner with our denomination's Division of Worldwide Ministries or with other traditional mission-sending agencies. Again, the MOA is requested for a specific project, a specific amount, and a specific time period.

Since designated giving has been encouraged, mission planning and implementation have expanded across all departmental lines. Our children's ministries department regularly plans specific mission outreach projects that will best attract children and their families. These mission projects are integrated with the teaching and ministry priorities of the department. Youth Mission and Ministry sponsors its own set of mission activities, such as the house-building project in Mexico. University Ministries sponsors World Deputation programs and deploys hundreds of university students in Christmas and spring break short-term mission outreaches. Periodically, new ministry-specific task forces are developed in order to support an active group of lay members who share a special commitment to a very specific and timely ministry outreach.

Our Bosnia Task Force was created when several lay members served in that war-torn country. They had witnessed the devastation war had caused and planned a way that our congregation could continue as a partner with a significant ministry working with war orphans and children suffering from the war's trauma. A Romanian Task Force developed from the concern that short-term team members brought back after serving Romanian orphans. Funds and missioners have been sent consistently to this program, all through the efforts of the task force. One very gifted woman formed a Russia Task Force to provide personnel and financial support to a whole range of mission activities the congregation has maintained with the Russian Orthodox Church in the Saint Petersburg area. The importance, however, is not in the location or nature of the project so much as it is the empowerment of people to make their mission contribution to those ministries that give them the greatest personal challenge.

Staff Ministry Accounts (SMA)

Have you ever heard, or perhaps even made the complaint yourself that, "Our church has too many staff members. Their salaries plus benefits consume too large a portion of our church budget." Some years ago, our session voted for a moratorium on the hiring of new staff. But the number of staff has almost doubled since then, and the moratorium has never been lifted! It was not necessary to lift the moratorium. We discovered a new way of presenting and funding ministry. If staff members are hired to *do* the work of ministry, then the complaint merits a hearing. However, if these additional staff members are employed for the purpose of expanding ministry and for mobilizing and equipping laity for leadership roles, then there needs to be a staff sufficient to meet these training needs and to keep volunteers spiritually healthy.

There are no absolute formulas that determine how large a church needs to be before it employs additional staff. The problem of adequate staffing is usually determined only by the amount of available resources in the congregation's budget, and there is *never* enough available to make the staff changes desired—at least not until the congregation begins to think more creatively. Under our old ways of thinking, staff salaries and benefits had grown to consume two thirds of the available financial resources of the congregation. Now we have a greatly enlarged staff, but a much smaller percentage of the available funds is needed to support this staff. Our staff size is large because our commitment to lay mobilization is so strong. Four hundred volunteers are needed to staff the children's ministry department, another 400 serve each week in urban outreach ministries, and 250 are involved in various global ministry task forces. The youth and university ministries need more than 150 volunteers each to staff their ministries. Experience has convinced us that it takes ministry professionals to support this large number of volunteers who are the ones most responsible for the various ministries of our congregation.

We had to develop a new strategy for funding additional staff if we were to continue expanding our ministry. The Staff Ministry Accounts (SMA) were initiated to allow any department to expand its outreach ministries by developing a personalized support mechanism for those with special interest in the ministry to financially support it. We eliminated the artificial difference between staff members involved in helping the congregation implement outreach ministries, and church members serving in traditional mission assignments outside the life of the congregation. The SMA are financially underwritten in the same way as the POA. This means for developing financial support has been very successful. Once the decision has been made to begin a new ministry and to employ a compensated staff person, we have enough assurance from our history of the congregation's supportive response that the new staff person receives full compensation from the first day of employment. God and the congregation have never let us down!

It makes little sense to send new missionaries ten thousand miles away while we neglect equally important ministry challenges at home. However, this should not become an either/or decision. By developing one more creative source of funding, both goals can be accomplished. Our mission challenge is one for our Jerusalem (Seattle) as well as one for the ends of the earth! We need to develop a strategy that will keep us faithful to our Lord's commission.

Special Mission Offerings

Our church members are generous people. When we created a positive environment of sound financial planning, and when we became creative in how we offered opportunities for response to ministry, congregational giving soared! We have found that, apart from receiving regular tithes and offerings at our regular worship services, special mission giving opportunities can be planned and promoted that excite and challenge the congregation. It is important to never take advantage of a congregation. Never build a culture of begging people for more! Rather, believe that your members are generous and extend to them additional opportunities for planned special offerings.

We have established five special mission offerings yearly. While focused on a particular department's mission activities, each is very specific in the mission cause for which funding is requested. When the members contribute, there is a very clear understanding of what will be accomplished by the funds generated from this particular offering. Our church had a longstanding tradition of receiving a Christmas Eve offering for missions. But when this "general mission offering" was made far more interesting and compelling by applying some marketing expertise to its presentation, the offering doubled, tripled, then tripled again in a matter of just a few years. People want to be generous, but they want some specificity in their giving. They need to know how their gift will make a difference. We maintain that same promotional link between contributor and contribution in each of these special offerings.

We began a process of reevaluating our special offerings by analyzing the church year according to seasonal interests, time-critical needs, and ministry opportunities. We then proposed a special offering calendar, which was agreed upon by the session.

The special offering year begins with an offering to support the spiritual ministries and house-building activities of our Department of Youth Mission and Ministry. Because this department sends out several hundred youth and parents in short-term mission assignments to Mexico, the whole congregation looks forward to participating in this special giving opportunity. Each Palm Sunday we receive our regular One Great Hour of Sharing offering, which goes to fund special mission projects for ministries to the pockets of need in our own community. The first Sunday of June, when students are on everyone's minds, the Department of University Ministries receives a special World Deputation offering to fund its summer and vacation student ministries. After children have gone back to school in the fall, our Department of Children's Ministries receives an early October offering for those mission projects of special interest to our children and their families. This has helped that department go way beyond serving just the spiritual and educational needs of our own children. Now they have a strong mission commitment to kids and families in our community who will not usually darken the doors of our churches. For example, this offering supports a new ministry to families visiting Seattle to care for the special health needs of their children confined to several area hospitals. We end the year with the Christmas Eve offering, which is received in all seven services. This offering always helps to fund new mission outreach projects locally and globally. Fifteen years ago, the two mission offerings received on Palm Sunday and Christmas Eve totaled less than twenty thousand dollars. Now with a comprehensive but balanced special offering plan, these five special offerings total more than a half million dollars! When offering results are reported to the congregation on subsequent Sunday worship services, the congregation usually breaks into a chorus of applause. When you can get a congregation that enthusiastic about giving, something very important and significant is happening! People want, people need to be generous. But they want to feel that their special gift will make a difference. These gifts have made an enormous difference in the scope and effectiveness of the congregation's mission outreach.

The Grace of Giving

It is easy to underestimate the willingness of parishioners to financially support ministries that engage their interest. If guilt and obligation are the prime motivators for giving, then our financial appeals have diminishing results. But when the leading edge of our appeal is opportunity—opportunities that the contributors have participated in creating—the results are surprising and rewarding.

During the apostle Paul's time, the Macedonian churches were a marvelous example of charitable giving. Great difficulties had come to the Jerusalem church. The church suffered intense persecution inflicted upon them by tyrannical Roman despots and religious zealots. Famine spread throughout the small Christian community. Paul acknowledges the Macedonian churches for their generous response to this need: "We want you to know about the grace that God has given Macedonian churches. Out of the most severe trial, their overflowing joy and their extreme poverty welled up in rich generosity. For I testify that they gave as much as they were able, and even beyond their ability. Entirely on their own, they urgently pleaded with us for the privilege of sharing in this service to the saints" (2 Corinthians 8:1–4). We need to do more in our congregations to cultivate this grace of giving. Here are a few helpful suggestions:

- *Trust* the members' generous impulses in contributing to those areas of ministry that best reflect their hearts' interest. They will still remember that the operational needs of the church must be provided for as well.
- *Challenge* the members to be faithful in their stewardship. "To whom much is given, much is required" is our standard for measurement.
- *Focus* stewardship challenges on creative and compelling outreach ministries. There is little interest in just meeting the need for underwriting budgets. Though budgets must be funded, they will be when we act wisely and trust the generosity of God's people.
- *Learn to risk* for the sake of God's kingdom, and never be surprised by the Lord's provision.
- *Cultivate* a spirit of gratitude and thankfulness in the hearts of your people.

11

Short-Term Mission:
Superficial or Strategic?

*J*im was an insurance broker with a lively interest in mission. He demonstrated this interest in a variety of ways. He served faithfully on various mission committees and served for one year as a volunteer at the U.S. Center for World Mission. Jim was generous in his financial support for various mission outreach programs. After Jim finished at the U.S. Center for World Mission, he participated in one of our short-term mission outreaches in Costa Rica. Upon his return he was highly motivated to consider future short-term mission assignments, including those of longer duration. He patiently waited for just the right opportunity. Sometime later when I needed a team leader for the church's ministry in Albania, Jim volunteered for one year of service. Jim's field responsibilities grew from providing leadership for our university ministry team to taking responsibility for organizing an ecumenical national Bible society. Jim's one-year commitment ended, but he stayed on for a second year and then a third. What had started as a ten-day short-term mission visit to Costa Rica had now expanded to three additional years of service in Albania.

Claudia was a member of our singles' ministry leadership team. She decided to participate in one of their short-term mission opportunities, one that would not require a long interruption from her job. Like Jim, she decided to volunteer for the next Vacation with a Purpose (VWAP) short-term mission to Costa Rica. Near the end of their Costa Rica experience they were paired up as a team to pray for one another while on assignment after they returned to Seattle. They even shared a couple of mementos to remind each other of their prayer covenant. Then Jim went off to Albania. Claudia, inspired by her brief mission experience, volunteered for another short-term mission assignment, this time with Latin America Mission's Christ for the Cities program, first in Costa Rica, then in Mexico, and finally with the large Hispanic population in the San Diego area. Her ten-day experience extended into four years of service! Later, Claudia joined our ministry team and provided leadership for a new, church-sponsored, short-term mission program, while Jim remained in Albania. However, the initial prayer commitment they made to each other in Costa Rica was revived on a visit Claudia and a friend made to Albania. Their friendship flourished, then was replaced by romance and then by marriage! Now Jim has resumed his insurance career and Claudia has chosen to be a stay-at-home mom caring for their beautiful new daughter. No short-term mission advocate can promise these results for every participant. But Jim and Claudia's story does illustrate the great results that can come from small investments!

Why Waste Money on Short-Term Mission?

I am a member of the American Society of Missiologists, a group of mission professors, denominational mission leaders, and mission agency executives. These members represent Roman Catholic, mainline Protestant, and evangelical mission organizations and institutions. We share a common concern and commitment to the mission of the church. At each yearly conference the program committee selects a specific mission theme as its focus. Papers are written and circulated in advance of the conference, then are presented at the annual gathering. Spirited discussions always follow the presentations! At one of the annual conferences, short-term mission was selected as the study theme. A lively and often heated discussion followed every major presentation. The majority of the issues raised concerned the validity and effectiveness of short-term mission.

"How can a short-term mission experience really be effective when the missioner knows neither the culture nor language of the host culture? Wouldn't our mission dollars be more wisely invested in supporting a few more mission projects or career missionaries and national workers who are prepared to remain in the field, learn the language and the culture, and thereby be far more effective in their ministries?" It soon became apparent that there was no consensus on how these mission leaders evaluated the effectiveness of short-term mission. Some perceived it as primarily a learning and sensitizing experience, and, indeed, short-term mission service can be a part of the spiritual formation of participants. Others saw it as an ineffective attempt to engage in more traditional mission service, only for a much briefer time. Still others argued that the negative impact of short-term mission on national church leaders and missionaries outweighed any positive benefits. These workers were already overburdened with their own mission responsibilities. They hardly needed their ministry interrupted in order to serve as tour hosts for groups of inexperienced but well-meaning mission activists. "Short-term missioners' intentions may be admirable, but their expectations and demands are quite unrealistic," some argued. "Short-termers do build houses, dig ditches, clean up slums, and plant gardens. But given the high cost of travel, the funds needed to pay for exporting sweat labor makes this type of expenditure questionable in some people's minds. This same work can be accomplished by hiring local labor at much lower costs, and it will help the local economy. Moreover, by hiring locals we empower them to accomplish their own project goals." If these types of arguments are the only criteria for measuring short-term mission effectiveness, then these activities do fall short of our mission goals. They are neither cost-effective nor culturally sensitive.

Educational Experience or Service Opportunity?

Fortunately, the debate does not end with these arguments. Additional criteria can be legitimately used to measure short-term mission effectiveness. With my extensive short-term mission experience, both in the field and in serving the congregation, I have developed a different set of evaluative tools from those developed by academics and administrators not directly engaged in parish ministries. Instead of focusing only upon those tasks accomplished in the host community, we should also measure the impact of the activity in the life of the missioner. We want to be able to evaluate the discipleship development experienced by the participant as well as the direct benefits to the local program. Participants and field project hosts need to share this understanding and be committed to the same goals. Short-term teams come to serve, but they also come to receive—to learn rather than to teach, to be and become rather than to work and to do. Through these cross-cultural service opportunities we hope that the short-termer will open up to a whole new set of realities and values. Rather than measuring home culture values against host culture values, the participant learns how to evaluate both home and foreign cultural values in contrast to the values of the kingdom of God.

One of the greatest goals of these limited cross-cultural experiences is for the participants to sort out their own cultural assumptions and to test them against new cultural values. Their exposure to a different cultural value system will help them do this. Before I lived among slum dwellers in Calcutta and tenant farmers in the Philippines, I thought it was the wealthy of the world who were generous. But in working with the poorest of the poor, I discovered in them a level of sacrificial sharing that was far greater than I had learned from my own affluent culture. The rich give out of their surplus; the poor give out of their poverty. When invited to their important family celebrations, I discovered that knowing how to give a party is not limited to those with surplus funds to spend. You have never been to a "real" party until you have celebrated life's most important passages—celebrations of birth, marriage, children, and even death—with these who have so little of this world's goods.

Cross-cultural learning experiences should never be limited to just a few mission specialists or highly trained professionals. We all need our lives to be transformed through cross-cultural service experiences. The call to follow Jesus Christ is a cross-cultural call! Responding to Jesus' invitation, receiving our citizenship in his kingdom, demands that we adopt a whole new set of values and priorities. These will be different and higher than those that are a part of our own culture. Consider the cross-cultural implications of these words of Jesus: "Seek first my kingdom, then food, housing, clothing, and longevity will follow. If you want to live, be ready to die. If you want to be exalted, humble yourself. If you wish to increase, decrease. If you want to save your life, lose it!" Each of these kingdom values directly challenges our own cultural values and assumptions. Our culture says, "Get ahead! Look out for yourself!" Participation in a well-planned cross-cultural mission has the potential for beginning a lifelong struggle with one's cultural values, which are often inconsistent with life in God's kingdom. In the process of this struggle we can separate what is traditional and cultural from what is invested with eternal value.

These mission experiences will contribute significantly to our spiritual renewal and development. They will transform us, convert us into becoming more obedient and faithful disciples of Christ. Well-planned short-term mission experiences will help participants

- develop personal awareness of their absolute dependence upon God;
- learn how to share their personal faith with others;
- understand more clearly the crosss-cultural Christ and his kingdom;
- understand more clearly the world Christ came to redeem;
- identify their false values and create awareness and space for new values;
- move from independence to interdependence;
- be open to the obedience and accountability of community;
- overcome their ideas of cultural superiority, provincialism, and false nationalism;
- build commitment for the unity and fellowship of the body of Christ;
- increase awareness of the importance and need for prayer;
- enhance their understanding of Christian vocation;
- be challenged to a life of sacrifice and service;
- learn how to *receive* in ministry rather than just to *give.*

These are but a few of the most obvious benefits participants may receive from short-term cross-cultural ministry. I have preached these values in sermons and taught them in lectures and conference addresses. I have written of these benefits and values. But the classroom of short-term mission service is a far more powerful instructor. Spiritual transformation that begins on a short trip can become a lifetime journey!

Vacation with a Purpose

During the mid-eighties our single adult ministry grew rapidly in number and became more diverse. Some singles came to form new relationships, others to join a support group that would help them to recover from a divorce, overcome an addiction, learn more from the Bible, or develop new ministry interests. Many of them had been very successful in business, deeply committed to their careers, but they were not feeling successful with life. In spite of their career success they felt that those things of greatest value were missing. These were seekers who, lacking purposeful direction in life and filled with questions regarding their current career paths, were open to new ideas and opportunities. Surplus income made it possible for them to travel, to take interesting vacations in exotic locations, to join health clubs, and to acquire more than just the bare necessities of life.

Sensing these unfulfilled needs, our leaders explored new ways to minister that could help meet these needs and utilize the resources of this talented group. Vacation with a Purpose (VWAP) was the result. VWAP was created to disciple young Christians through experiences directly related to travel. The program was designed to provide short-term mission experiences, usually of one or two weeks' duration. During this brief vacation, participants would encounter a new culture and build new friendships. Sharing life with other teammates while living in difficult situations would help build community among the participants.

One of the earliest VWAP trips was to an orphanage south of Ensenada, Mexico. Since that first trip, hundreds more adults, mostly young and single, have joined this special mission experience. Subsequent teams have ministered in Mexico, Haiti, Costa Rica, France, Guatemala, Mississippi, and Hawaii. Why would these participants spend their personal funds and use their accumulated vacation time to participate in a VWAP mission? What motivates them to forgo pleasure vacations and commit to travel-work experiences in their place? These trips are not to the world's glamorous locations but to tough places where human need is overwhelming and conveniences for the traveler are nonexistent.

The desire to experience community and the deep longing for purpose motivates these participants to join even before the spiritual benefits of a trip are clear. The success of Vacation with a Purpose can be measured in the lives of those who have returned to their careers as spiritually transformed people, and in the lives of those who have experienced VWAP as the first step in discovering new opportunities for continuing mission service. These results have little to do with the particular work project these participants join while in their host country. Instead, transformation takes place through the relationships that are formed, the community they become part of, and the diversity of experiences they share.

Taking the Journey

Values and needs change. Cultures are always in transition. Needs and opportunities that challenged one generation are not the same as those that motivate today's generation. Therefore, we have shifted our focus from vacation and action to a short-term mission experience more centered in spiritual formation and discipleship. Young adults in this new millennium are more concerned with the inner journey and less with the outer journey. "Journey" is a newer short-term team ministry program designed to help meet these needs for spiritual growth and maturity. We describe the experience as one of going, growing, learning, and serving through cross-cultural ministries. Journey participants include adults and families, and a broad spectrum of people is included: from those who are well-seasoned in their Christian commitment to those who are just beginning to discover life when it is lived with Jesus Christ as Lord. All participants commit in advance to the goals and purposes of the mission. They are placed on teams of three or more, with leaders who are people of a vibrant and infectious faith. The short-term experience is cross-cultural in nature and lasts from a few days to one month. Ministry teams work with their field hosts in a partnership of mutual respect. Team members are required to commit to predeparture training, on-site involvement, and posttrip debriefing. After they return from their field experience, participants are encouraged to seek out ways to continue on their journey of faith.

One of the unique aspects of Journey is that it makes a significant impact on the congregation's other mission projects. Rather than selecting ministry sites at random, these sites are carefully selected to support existing mission projects. These team efforts strengthen our mission partnerships and often become the training ground for longer-term mission service.

You Can Travel with a Difference

I have sometimes struggled with the idea of spending money on unnecessary or frivolous travel. When there are so many career missionaries waiting to go to the field but lack the funding, and when there are many worthy mission projects that are underfunded, it seems that it might be better stewardship to discourage this type of travel. Instead, we could encourage individuals to use their resources to fund these mission needs. This is an idealistic idea but one that has never seemed to be compelling or marketable!

With further reflection on the issue, however, I have reevaluated my approach. After all, most Americans have discretionary income that they can spend on travel and recreation. But how many times can one person go to Disneyland in a single lifetime? Some of our travel and vacation plans seem to have more to do with conquering our boredom than quenching our desires to see new places and to meet new friends. Why not offer people travel opportunities that would provide them with more spiritual meaning than the average vacation? Travel with a Difference (TWAD) was created to meet this objective.

Participants in TWAD are called pilgrims rather than tourists. They are invited to take a journey, often one that is difficult and sometimes unnerving. TWAD does not take participants to the usual tourist spots or the finest five-star hotels. This travel experience helps participants to gain greater understanding of poverty, disease, social injustice, and spiritual darkness. It is designed to help them wrestle with difficult questions: What are the causes of these problems, the gross injustices so many suffer? Are there any solutions to these problems? Does God really care about the physical, social, and economic problems that affect his creation?

TWAD is the beginning of a journey rather than a destination. Its goals are clearly understood before the pilgrim commits to travel. These goals include:

1. To develop a more realistic understanding of our affluence and the responsibilities inherent in our possessing so much, but without inducing fear, false guilt, or despair.

2. To deepen personal and corporate feelings of compassion for the world's impoverished and oppressed people, and to help participants learn to humbly serve and be served by those less privileged than they are.
3. To develop a greater sensitivity toward ministering in partnership with the churches and Christians in the host country, and to assist participants in discovering the joy of sharing Christ's love within the context of these newly formed incarnational relationships.
4. To develop a clearer understanding of the spiritual, physical, and social needs of people living in the two-thirds world, and to help participants develop a deeper appreciation for the wisdom, values, and priorities of these people who are often poor in material possessions but rich in spiritual values.
5. To encourage participants' growth as disciples of Jesus Christ and in their relationship with those of their own culture who accompany them on the journey.
6. To encourage participants to enter into a discipling-discipled relationship with the poor Christians they serve and are served by.

The pilgrims begin their preparations by attending several sessions of orientation and training. On the day of departure, the first stage of community building begins with a Communion service in the airport chapel. Then all board the plane, headed toward those destinations planned for the journey. A typical pilgrimage includes Thailand, Nepal, Bangladesh, and Calcutta, India. Another focuses on some of the former communist countries of Eastern Europe or Central Asia. A third takes pilgrims to the ancient Christian lands of Turkey, Greece, and Egypt. Each of these locations becomes a place for rich learning experiences. In each location we have mission partners with whom the congregation has been involved for many years. Each day provides a balance of learning experiences, personal and team worship, and participation in work projects with mission partners. "Seminars in the Field" provide education in mission, social outreach ministry, biblical perspectives on poverty, and general country orientation. The work projects are all requested by and prearranged with our field partners.

The final stage of the overseas portion of the program is a time for reflection, recreation, and renewal. It takes place at a resort-type hotel where two or three days are spent digesting, assimilating, and integrating the experience. The pilgrims are encouraged to spend extended periods of time in silence each day. At the end of the day, they gather for guided discussions concerning their experiences. Play and leisure activities are an important part of the recreation that follows! Then the evenings conclude with worship and prayer. A TWAD trip is designed to help each participant deal with this question: "How will all I have learned and experienced during this pilgrimage fit into the rest of my life?" New creative alternatives are mutually explored. One's service for Christ and his kingdom takes on new meaning, meaning more full of "wordly" wisdom and understanding, and infused with fresh hope and joy!

A New Time, A New Journey, A New Need!

Christ's commission is for the *whole* church to take the *whole* gospel to the *whole* world! Every member is called to participate in mission; therefore, we need to provide a broad range of opportunities. With its diverse range of practical hands-on experiences, short-term mission can be an effective tool in assisting any congregation, small or large, to fulfill its unique role in this Great Commission. If your church does not have the resources to develop its own short-term mission ministry, then seek out those specialized agencies with short-term mission service as their expertise. Form partnerships with other small churches or with your denomination's associations that will help you do together what you cannot accomplish alone. Many opportunities are available to help your congregation use short-term mission as a more effective part of its mission witness and service. These short-term mission experiences will greatly expand the mission vision of your congregation, and because of the excitement generated by personal involvement in mission outreach, the congregation's resources available to *do* mission will likewise grow.

12

Partnership in Mission

Webster's Dictionary defines partnership as "a shared relationship, an association formed voluntarily in order to carry out a particular enterprise." *Partnership* comes from the Anglo-French word *parcener,* an old legal term denoting "co-heirship." The scriptures remind us that we are partners, "heirs of God and co-heirs with Christ" (Romans 8:17). The AD 2000 and Beyond movement's director, Luis Bush, defines partnership as "an association of two or more autonomous bodies who have formed a trusting relationship, and fulfill agreed-upon expectations by sharing complementary strengths and resources, to reach their mutual goal." In today's world, networking is the new relational standard for individuals, congregations, and corporations. Jets accelerate our travel, computers facilitate and speed the exchange of information. National borders have become irrelevant with the World Trade Organization's policies among partner nations. Empowered partnerships make it possible for us to accomplish together what was impossible to accomplish in earlier times. These new partnerships become critically important in mission today, whether they are the partnerships of churches, mission societies, or major organizations.

In his second letter to the Corinthian church, Paul reminded these believers of the important partnership that had developed between the churches in Macedonia and the church at Jerusalem. This partnership emerged out of the suffering of Jerusalem Christians. At the time of his writing they were suffering from serious famine and oppression. "We want you to know about the grace that God has given the Macedonian churches. . . . [T]hey urgently pleaded with us for the privilege of sharing in this service to the saints" (2 Corinthians 8:1, 4). This concern shaped a partnership of sharing. Where once the Jerusalem church was responsible for sending out good news—the bread of life—to those in distant provinces of the Roman Empire, now these new Christians were sending offerings to purchase bread to alleviate the suffering of the Jerusalem Christians.

Principles for Healthy Partnerships

During the years I served as president of World Concern, I learned more about partnership than I had learned while serving as an overseas church-planting missionary or a stateside pastor. World Concern was in the business of relief and development. We defined these activities in a way that helped us understand partnership. *Relief* is doing something for people who cannot do it for themselves. *Development* is the process of coming alongside people and helping them help themselves. These newly empowered people are then better able to discover their unique gifts, talents, and resources. In mobilizing these gifts, talents, and resources, these people help themselves to meet whatever development challenges they face. This is why development is referred to in terms of self-help. However, partnership is more than self-help. Partnership is when two individuals or groups make available to each other certain resources that will help them accomplish together what neither could accomplish alone.

In working alongside people who have suffered from severe want and hunger, oppression and injustice, or dislocations resulting from wars or natural disasters, I have learned a great deal about partnership. Without creative partnerships, both within the community and with other organizations and agencies outside of the community, it was impossible to accomplish much of significance. I learned an important truth I had not known before: Every person has *needs,* and every person possesses *resources* to help meet those needs. Discovering this basic principle of development encouraged me to form partnerships that would contribute positively to all who chose to participate. In a healthy partnership, each partner has something of value to contribute while receiving from the other a needed resource. These same principles I learned from doing relief and development work are of equal importance as we conduct our traditional mission activities. The task of world evangelization and church development is far too important to trust only to one person, congregation, or organization. And it is far too important to trust to one nationality of workers. We truly need each other!

Our congregation has been greatly enriched through a variety of mission partnerships. We partner with national churches, training institutions, and mission organizations in the field. In more recent years our congregation has learned how to successfully partner with our presbytery and our denomination's Division of Worldwide Ministries. This has enhanced our congregation-based mission initiatives. Because of our own program arrogance, an arrogance that all too often characterizes megachurches, for years we acted as though our mission efforts could be just as effective without these denominational relationships. But by working cooperatively in partnership, we influence and enrich each other's mission efforts. The Presbyterian Church (U.S.A.) has more than two hundred years of fruitful mission experience. However, sometimes in this day of individualism and entrepreneurism we feel that there is nothing for us to learn from history. But history tends to repeat itself. (The only thing we learn from history is that no one learns from history!) Observing many contemporary mission efforts, I discover many enthusiastic but individualistic missionaries and mission leaders who are ill-informed by history. As a consequence, they tend to repeat the same mistakes in implementing their mission programs that older mission organizations have already made and have already learned from.

We have avoided some of those mistakes by learning from the experience of others. A group of pastors created the Association of Presbyterian Mission Pastors, an organization for the purpose of fostering these important relationships and partnerships among mission-mobilized congregations and between local congregations and the denomination's mission organization. Our congregation's mission program has also been enriched through forming partnerships between our congregation and selected parachurch ministries that help us to be more effective and more holistic in our mission activities. We have learned a great deal about spiritual formation in partnerships we have formed with Orthodox and Roman Catholic Christians. The richness of their mission history and their understanding of spirituality have often been ignored by Western Protestant churches. We have allowed our theological and ecclesiastical differences to prevent us from working together in areas of ministry where these differences do not need to separate us. We both suffer as a result of this separation. Likewise, differences between pentecostals and noncharismatics, separatists and inclusivists, independents and mainliners unnecessarily separate us from working together where it is possible and could be profitable for our joint mission endeavors.

Four Distinguishing Marks of Effective Partnerships

In effective partnerships, there are at least four distinguishing characteristics that will help make the partnership an empowering and satisfying relationship. First, effective partnerships are infused with a strong commitment to *mutuality*. If one partner does all the giving while the other partner is only receiving, or if one partner makes all the decisions while the other partner plays a more passive role, that partnership is seriously lacking in mutuality.

Our congregation formed what we thought was a healthy partnership with the Divya Shanti Association, located in Bangalore, India. This church community had developed a marvelous balance between evangelism and social action. They conducted a very effective training program where invited guest volunteers received practical training in the theology of holistic ministry and the principles of effective community development. Some of our best mission volunteers had benefited greatly from this program. After we had worked in this "partnership" for several years, one day I received a call from the project's director, an Anglican canon, Dr. Vinay Samuel. He called to remind us that there should be more to our partnership than their receiving our funding in exchange for their training our mission candidates. "We are willing to continue receiving and training your church's volunteers. But I am wondering if you are ready and willing to receive and train one of our lay leaders?" Isn't it fascinating, that in a certain false humility some Western churches have developed, we tend to overcompensate for our aggressive and nationalistic attitudes and conduct by thinking that we have nothing of worth to bring to the table! Vinay explained that he had a church member, a middle-aged woman who was serving as headmistress of a successful girls school in Bangalore, who had dreamed for years that some day she might have the opportunity to serve as a missionary in Africa. Upon learning of her desire to be trained by us for this service, I accepted the challenge.

Jothi Parker came to Seattle and learned from us various forms and principles of ministry. (And we learned from her!) After her year of training was over, she fulfilled that long-term dream of mission service in Africa. For her first term, she served under a partnership we formed with the Church of South India as her missionary sending body, and the British Church Mission Society and the Anglican Church of the Province of Kenya as the receiving body. University Presbyterian Church became her primary funding source. After four years of successful ministry, she returned for a second four-year term to serve the Anglican churches in Tanzania. Finally, after three full terms of service she returned to her home in Bangalore and began a delayed retirement!

The second characteristic of successful partnership is probably the most difficult to achieve—*sufficiency.* The American church is so accustomed to operating from the perspective of our own strength that we develop an attitude of omnicompetence—we can do anything and accomplish everything. We need nothing from others in order to meet our needs. Paul gives us a powerful reminder of the importance of interdependence in his commendation of the Philippian church for its generosity. He reminds the Philippians that while today they have the resources and others have the need, they should prepare themselves for a great reversal! In some future time it may very well be that the Jerusalem church, currently suffering, will use its resources to meet the needs of future Philippian Christians. Attitudes

of self-sufficiency never foster healthy partnership relationships. All parties engaging in partnership must have a
clear understanding that their sufficiency is only a healthy
attitude when it recognizes its interdependence with others. Ultimately our sufficiency is rooted in our dependence upon God. We see this healthy interdependence
elsewhere in scripture: "He who gathered much did not
have too much, and he who gathered little did not have too
little" (2 Corinthians 8:15).

Partnerships that endure the test of time will be char-
acterized by *maturity*. No partnership will long survive
with stereotyped roles of junior partner and senior partner. Working together will bring maturity to and respect
for each cooperating partner.

While teaching at the Oxford Centre for Mission Studies, I was greatly influenced by the thinking of Dr. Kwame
Bediako, who served as theological responder to the lectures. Dr. Bediako leads the Presbyterian Center for
Mission Studies in Accrapong, Ghana. In one of his
responses, he shared a series of fictional exchanges he had
authored. It was written as a dialogue between two mission partners. One partner was an American congregation,
highly mobilized for mission and possessing an overwhelming desire to do good. The other partner was a
developing indigenous church. This exchange was the
basis for some lively discussion among our multinational
students. They were helpful to me to better understand
healthy partnerships, especially when one partner has far
more tangible resources than the other partner. Here are
his letters:

Dear African church:

*Greetings from America, a land blessed by Almighty
God! We are delighted by the way you have developed
and matured as a native African church under the gifted*

leadership of American missionaries, including some from our very own church.

As a testimony of our generous care for you, we are proposing to send you a brand new four-wheel-drive Ford Bronco, a great achievement of American technology that we are certain you will find of great value in your splendid ministry. Living in such an underdeveloped society, we know that this gift will have special meaning for you.

Your loving brothers and sisters from America

Dear American brothers and sisters:

Thank you for your most generous offer to send us a Ford Bronco. Your offered sacrifice is deeply appreciated. Could we request you, however, to consider sending us some sturdy bicycles rather than the Ford Bronco?

Our pastors are often without any means of transportation, and in order to visit the scattered churches under their leadership they have to walk many miles, which often requires long absences from home and family. Furthermore, several years ago we were sent an American Jeep, but this gift was not altogether a success. Our bishop claimed it for his transportation needs and when he retired it became the personal possession of his family, and the church has never had any use of it since.

With heartfelt gratitude,
Your loving partners in Africa

Dear partners in Africa:

We are responding quickly to your most recent letter. To say the least, we are extremely disappointed that you do not wish us to send the Ford Bronco. We happen to know that it is the finest land transportation available. We had already placed an order for one with a special discount. One of the members of our mission committee owns the local Ford dealership. We have a talented artist in our congregation who had already donated his valuable time and talent to design pictures of our church and our beloved senior pastor that we had painted on the front doors of the vehicle. The designs are great but are hardly appropriate to be painted on the handlebars of bicycles!

However, we are arranging the purchase of fifty bicycles and we will write you when they are ready for shipment.

Your loving friends in America

Dear American sisters and brothers:

With great joy and thankfulness we announced your most generous gift of fifty bicycles at our regional synod meeting last week. There was loud and spontaneous shouts of praise to our Lord for a gift that will be so useful for the Lord's work. This gift will benefit many of our pastors who would need to walk to their outreach ministries without the provision of a bicycle.

Our church would like very much to send you a gift in return. Our region is famous for its handicrafts, and we would be honored to send some to your church members. Please let us know if you would prefer mats with our tribal designs woven into them or some woodcarvings depicting native life in our village. Our pastor is also preparing to record a special series of Bible expositions with some of our original native music as background. Share these with your mission committee members or place them in your church library.

Our loving appreciation and fervent prayers are sent to each one of you.

Your loving brothers and sisters from Africa

Dear friends:

We are writing to request you not to think of sending gifts to us. Our congregation is a wealthy one and we would not want to receive anything from you that might make you poorer than you already are. And through past experience, we have found that most native handicrafts are not practical or of the right color combination for our modern homes.

Please tell your pastor not to bother sending us his Bible exposition and native music tapes. Our senior pastor is a most gifted Bible expositor and is author of no less than ten books of daily devotions. His last book on the topic of Christian humility was at the very top of the religious booksellers' list for two months!

The bicycles are almost ready for shipment and we will inform you as soon as we know their expected date of arrival in your country. We have shipped them by sea in order to save shipping costs, so they will probably not arrive for many months.

Christian greetings to you all!

The members and friends of your American partner church

An African Church's Telegraphed Response:
Dear American brothers and sisters:
Please cancel the shipment of bicycles. We do not think we should receive from those who will not receive from us.

Your disappointed brothers and sisters in your African partner church

Empowerment means that there will be an equitable and healthy sharing of power within the partnership. In empowered relationships there are no exclusive givers and takers. There are neither the strong nor the weak. Mutually developed and implemented program goals and objectives joined together with clearly defined responsibilities and delegated authority will create accountable and empowered partnerships. Without the full empowerment of each partner, our best partnerships will fail.

When promising the gift of the Holy Spirit to his disciples, Jesus spoke of empowerment. He promised them that they would have more than enough power to accomplish their enormous task of world evangelization: "You will receive power when the Holy Spirit comes on you; and you will be my witnesses . . . to the ends of the earth" (Acts 1:8). His promise is just as relevant for us today. As we participate in the power of his Spirit we are set free to empower others for shared ministry.

The Exciting
Possibilities of Partnership

Partnerships can be compared to two individuals performing on the flying trapeze. You have to be willing to leave the security of your trapeze to meet the person coming toward you from the other trapeze. Flying from one trapeze to the arms of your partner is sometimes a frightening prospect. But grasping your partner, after that free fall through space, is the ultimate thrill!

The element of risk in our partnerships causes us a great deal of uncertainty. Sometimes it brings pain. Something must be given up in order to gain something of greater value. Ministry partnerships can be compared to healthy marriages. Marriage compromised my independence! As a married man, I need to confer with another before making important decisions. Before marriage I was able to make my own decisions. But now my decisions impact more than me! At first, marriage threatened my self-confidence! I knew I could handle life alone quite well, thank you. But I have slowly learned to share responsibility for the well-being of my marriage partner. This is why marriage contributes significantly to sharpening one's negotiating skills! I have learned how to negotiate, confront, compromise, and sometimes yield! After

forty-seven years, marriage is still teaching me interdependence. Building a healthy and successful marriage is
a lifetime process. The same is true for enduring mission
partnerships. As long as the partnership lasts, there will be
new challenges to be resolved or understood and new part-
nerings skills that will need to be developed. But there
will also be newly shared achievements to celebrate.

A Word of Advice to Mission Committees

As your congregation serves in mission, be sure to look
both within and without to discover possible partnerships.
Church mission committees that understand their role to
be the custodian of all mission resources and energy will
not succeed in developing positive internal partnerships.
The Committee "door" is the one that must be entered if
any member plans to participate in mission. The committee becomes the repository of all mission learning and
experience. It is the keeper of all mission and missionary
relationships. "If you want to *do* mission come to us!"
Remember those qualities that define healthy partnerships: equality, mutuality, sufficiency, and empowerment.
These qualities will enhance our internal mission efforts
just as much as they do our external efforts. Let those program and policy guidelines that were established by mission committees *inform* your mission activities rather than
control the creative mission efforts of others. When developing reasoned and reasonable mission policies and procedures, be sure to implement these in ways that will
assist other groups within the congregation to engage in
mission. Do not allow them to become obstructions to
others' mission efforts. Empower participants to implement their vision for mission rather than merely expecting them to support the committee's vision. As a wise
leader, find your place on the sidelines and cheer the

efforts of others! These positive attitudes will help empower the whole congregation to become an all-church team committed to doing mission. There should be no lone rangers in the kingdom of God. Jesus first commissioned his disciples for ministry and sent them out two by two. As we effectively partner, we both teach and learn from one another, we both give and receive. We can each contribute funds, personnel, creative ideas, and program implementation. One plants, another waters, and God gives the increase.

Epilogue

*C*elebrations for what some called "the greatest event in one thousand years" have recently been observed. On January 1, A.D. 2000, a new century *and* a new millennium began. Governments, businesses, media companies, social service agencies, and churches had been planning for this event for decades. Six thousand members of the Millennium Society chartered the *Queen Elizabeth II,* transporting eighteen hundred passengers from New York to Alexandria, Egypt. In the suburbs of Cairo they bid farewell to the old millennium and ushered in the new at the base of the Great Pyramid of Cheops. Similar events took place around the world in the moonlit brightness of the Taj Mahal, at Mount Everest's base camp, along the slopes of Mount Kilimanjaro, at the Great Wall of China, and in darkness alongside Australia's Alice Rock. On the other hand, millennial celebrations in Seattle were cancelled because of the fear of terrorism. The people of most nations hoped for a new millennium that would be filled with new possibilities and a secure peace.

How great the changes were that occurred during the final few decades of the previous millennium! Travel during this jet age has made its impact on world mission. E-mail and other forms of communication have revolutionized how we are able to participate in mission. The ways we communicate, our methods of learning, the location of the workplace, all of these have been radically redefined and relocated by the computer. Computers have changed the way the world conducts its business, and mission outreach has not been left unaffected. New mission models of networking and partnership formation are the unplanned-for result of this new global society. Those who engage in world mission perceive the impact of a globalized economy as both blessing and potential curse. Despite all of these achievements and technological advances, we enter this new millennium with many of the old problems and threats still unresolved. Our world is experiencing a growing divide between Christians and Muslims. The gap between the rich and the poor continues to widen. While some Western economies decline, the economies of the new economic tigers of Asia expand. Massive sociological changes, accompanied by growing ecological and population crises, threaten all life on this planet. We wonder what the next millennium will bring.

In the closing years of the previous millennium we experienced the transformation of the church as well. In global mission, the torch has been passed, not so much to a new generation as to a whole new group of mission-mobilized national churches. Churches begun through the efforts of Western missionaries are now in the forefront of sending their own cross-cultural missionaries. Koreans, Brazilians, Filipinos, Nigerians, and Costa Ricans serve in mission outreach worldwide. Megachurches are able to achieve in mission outreach what only denominational and large interdenominational mission societies could achieve heretofore. There are conflicting predictions concerning mainline Protestant churches. Some predict their continued decline while others foresee a whole new renaissance of spiritual and numerical growth. Encouragingly, both inside and outside these historic denominations there is an evangelical surge that is reshaping the church in the West. Ministry loyalties are rooted much more in common values of ministry and beliefs rather than in those denominational and nondenominational structures that dominated the church scene in the twentieth century.

In the new millennium the pace of change will only accelerate. There will be a greater need for better prepared young leadership. These leaders will need a high degree of cultural awareness and sensitivity. The new millennium will require church leaders who are creative entrepreneurs and risk-takers. Women and men entrusted with leadership responsibilities will need to be flexible and innovative, highly relational people who are effective communicators. With a dominant global culture that is both secular and humanistic, the church will require leaders who are godly, Spirit-controlled, and who, in an age of increasing moral relativism, are deeply grounded in God's unchanging truth. The twenty-first–century church will need great thinkers, students, and scholars who by their own commitment to scholarship will discipline the thinking of the church. In the final decades of the twentieth century the church produced better ministry activists than great thinkers, thinkers equipped to deal seriously with some of the critical intellectual challenges of our day. Mark Noll, Wheaton College professor and author of the book, *The Scandal of the Evangelical Mind,* writes that at the cusp of the new millennium, "our evangelical ethos is activist, populist, pragmatic and utilitarian." N. K. Clifford, a brilliant Canadian scholar, summarizes the problem this way: "The evangelical Protestant mind has never relished complexity. Indeed its crusading genius, whether in religion or politics, has always tended toward an over-simplification of issues and the substitution of inspiration and zeal for critical analysis and serious reflection. The limitations of such a mind-set were less apparent in the relative simplicity of a rural frontier society." But those charged with leadership responsibilities in this new millennium will lead in a globalized society. The opportunities for success and the possibilities for failure are very great!

In the dawning of the new millennium we face new challenges, new frontiers in mission. They will require us to develop new strategies and create new partnerships. They will require new ways of thinking. Charles Malik, a Lebanese diplomat and leading Eastern Orthodox scholar, speaks wisely on our Western propensity toward ministry activism and points out some of the problems this activism creates: "The problem is not only to win souls but to save minds. If you win the whole world and lose the mind of the world, you will soon discover you have not won the world. Indeed, it may turn out that you have actually lost the world."

American young people, in particular those who are mission enthusiasts, often are in such a hurry to complete their university studies that they miss their education! They are eager to begin serving in mission and preaching the gospel, but sometimes place little value on learning from the greatest minds and souls of the past. J. Gresham Machen, the celebrated Presbyterian Bible scholar, remarked to the youth of his day, who were struggling through the disruptions of a major theological schism: "We may preach with all the fervor of a reformer, and yet succeed only in winning a straggler here and there. If we permit the whole collective thought of the nation or of the world to be controlled by ideas which, by the resistless force of logic, prevent Christianity from being regarded as anything more than a harmless delusion, what is today a matter of academic speculation, begins tomorrow to move armies and pull down empires." The Reformed revivalist Jonathan Edwards said, "The reason for exercising our intelligence is to know more of God and His loving ways with the world. For a Christian, the mind is important because God is important!" It will require the most trained and disciplined minds coupled with the passion and Spirit of God for us to engage the world with the gospel message in this new millennium. Mission service is not the place for the intellectual novice or the undisciplined activist. Mission in the new millennium will require the very best that our youth, our congregations, our church can give!

We are the generation alive and working in mission at the beginning of this new millennium. We are also the witnesses to the death of the last millennium. This moment in time comes but once every thousand years. What prophetic significance there may or may not be to the end and beginning of a millennium, to the year A.D. 2000, I will leave for others' speculation. I would rather face the new millennium with this comforting promise: "The Lord is not slow in keeping his promise, as some understand slowness. He is patient with you, not wanting anyone to perish, but everyone to come to repentance" (2 Peter 3:9).

God's patience requires us to look beyond the year A.D. 2000. God's patience will encourage us to trust fully his timing for completing the task of world evangelization. We can become so caught up in speculation concerning the importance of the time of his coming that we become overwhelmed with the present task that is before us. Or we may become overconfident in our strategies and overburdened with the proliferation of plans to "complete the task." Our God-given responsibility is not to finish the job, but it is to remain faithful to the task. Long-distance runners must be careful not to burn out. There is always the danger of peaking too soon and not finishing the race. Churches plan and strategize for the long run. Momentum is great, but thoughtful reflection regarding mission motivation and methods is critically important. We are called to faithfulness, not to fruitfulness. Let's not forget who is responsible for the fruit in our mission efforts! Always remember that in every time and generation, the church exists for mission as fire exists by burning. At the very center of mission is the local congregation, empowered by the Spirit, with its laity mobilized for the unfinished task.